A Yank Down Under

From America's Heartland to Australia's Outback

A Yank Down Under

From America's Heartland to Australia's Outback

by

Ray A. Wyatt

Sunflower University Press®
1531 Yuma • P. O. Box 1009 • Manhattan, Kansas 66505-1009 USA

Printed in the United States of America on acid-free paper.

Cover: American servicemen during an air raid on Darwin, Australia, June 20, 1943. Ray Wyatt is on the right wearing a World War I helmet. *Ray Wyatt photo*

Layout by Lori L. Daniel

ISBN 0-89745-228-3

Sunflower University Press is a wholly-owned subsidiary of the non-profit 501(c)3 Journal of the West, Inc.

For my three sons — Rob, Bill, and Tom — and my daughter, Ginny Rae, who won't have to listen to "yet another" of Dad's war stories.

They won't have to wonder what Dad did during the Big War.

It's all here.

Contents

Staff Sergeant Ray Wyatt USAFIA (United States Armed Forces in Australia), *ca.* 1943.

Australia

I love the Land Down Under
"Ah-strile-ya" and its clime,
Where the Outback is far out
And livin' is so sublime.

Home of the platypus and 'roo.
The "billy" can and mutton stew.
Fields of opal and yellow gold
And of minerals yet untold.

I love the "digger" and his "mite."
Always sure that "She'll be right."
I loved the Top End and the rain;
The jolly swagman's sweet refrain.

It's the land of "footy" and cool beer
A Melbourne Cup that's run each year.
Where a bloke has a "Fair dinkum go."
In a land that's still on the grow.

Ray Wyatt

P.S. There's a reef and a gold coast, too.
Australians will welcome you.

Acknowledgments

MOST WRITERS recognize their wife's contribution to their works so that they can go on living. I really mean it. Without my wife's input and encouragement I could not have offered the world this record of experiences.

Virginia has a degree in Education from Kansas State University, Manhattan, and was a Librarian at Camelback High School in Phoenix, Arizona, for nearly 20 years.

Thanks 'Ginia! You can use the computer now.

Preface

FIFTY YEARS AFTER serving as an intercept operator in 1942, attached to General Douglas MacArthur's Headquarters in Melbourne, Australia, I found that I had performed an important job there copying the Japanese *Katakana* secret code for the Signal Intelligence Service. SIS was on the leading edge of deciphering and cryptanalyzing secret codes that allowed the Allies in Europe and the Southwest Pacific to know every move of the Axis powers. Intelligence is vital before battles begin or troops and supplies are committed, and early in the war I had contributed, albeit unknowingly, to the success of the Pacific campaign.

I found my diary and notes that I had scribbled on pieces of paper while in combat zones in Australia and in the jungles of New Guinea. I don't remember carrying them around — and nearly 100 photo negatives — for three years while overseas, or even bringing them home with me.

One of the unconscious yet ironical aspects of war is the fact that those doing the fighting seldom know what is happening in the front next to them, or who is winning at any given moment. They tend to feel at the time that they are the only ones getting blasted and the only ones fighting. Weeks after the action, they hear from often unreliable sources about the losses and successes of campaigns around the world or in their own outfit.

Now, a half-century later, encouraged by my wife and children, I decided to write and explain my part in the conflict.

This book takes the reader back to a period when the United States was still recovering from the devastations of the drought and the Great Depression of the "Dirty '30s." It is a view through a window of time when Americans were optimistic and building stability in their lives and the national attitude was in a "go" situation. It begins at a time when a disgruntled German soldier named Adolf Hitler was bent on avenging his country's defeat in World War I, two decades earlier, and when a little guy called Hideki Tojo wanted all of the Pacific Ocean for himself.

Few Americans have heard or read of the war in the Northern Territory of Australia where nearly a quarter-million Allied servicemen served.

My story is not about bloodshed in battles or the gory side of war, but about new adventures in the life of a Kansas farm boy thrust into World War II in the early 1940s. It is about Australia — the land down under the equator — the land of the "digger" and the platypus, the jolly swagman, and the "'roos." It's about New Guinea, too.

Perhaps my World War II experiences will fill in one more piece of the total picture.

Chapter 1

Before Pearl Harbor

"IS THIS THE Yankee switch in Darwin?"

"This is Sergeant Wyatt — U.S. Army switchboard. Go ahead."

"A civilian white man has stolen the lubra away from the headman of the aborigines. The natives are about to riot. If you would get Constable McFarland to call Sergeant Tiernan, the Provost Marshal at Batchelor Field, would be much obliged. I am about 100 miles south of Darwin on the north-south track to Alice Springs."

I called the Australian Army switchboard and gave them the message. A voice answered back. "My bloody oath! Wouldn't it?"

A strange reply. It was from an Australian soldier and the first message I took as chief operator of a U.S. Army radio station in the Northern Territory of Australia in World War II.

Alone in a below-ground signal station in the bombed-out city of Darwin, Australia, the only sound was the hum of a 100-watt transmitter and the static from my Hallicrafter receiver. I wondered what

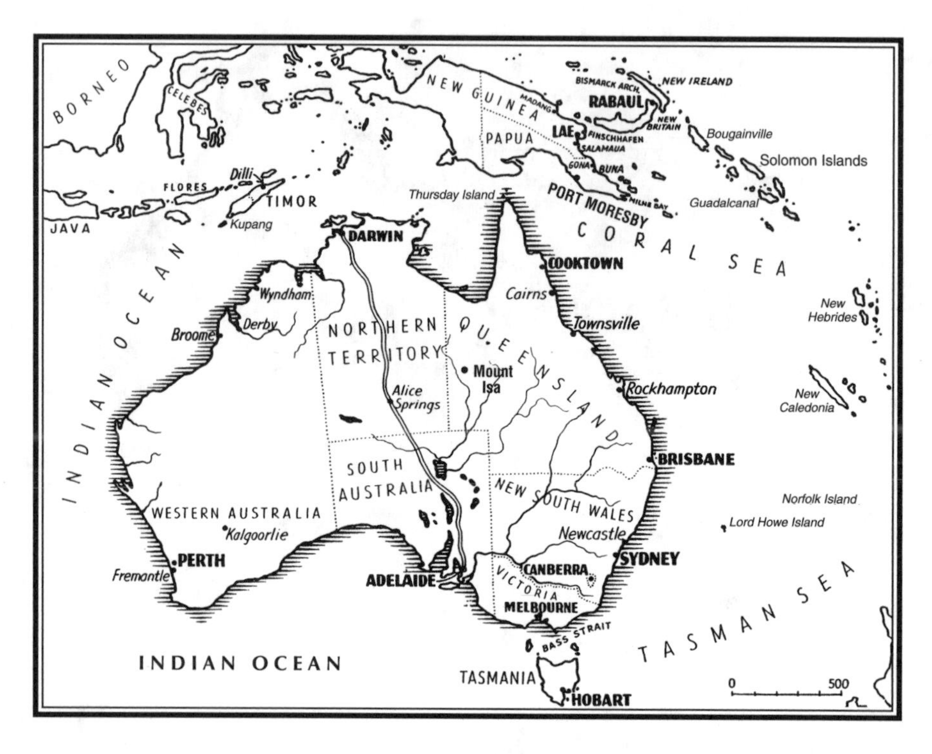

was going on. The war was against the Japanese wasn't it? Who were the aborigines? Where in the world was I?

It was 2200 hour, April 19, 1942.

I was in Arnhem Land along the northwest coast of Australia, home of the country's aborigines, their primitive man — a nomadic people living in the great deserts and bush country of Australia's top end. The aborigines may have been here for some 40,000 years. Now, as a great war threatened them, they had gone "bush" down the only road north and south through central Australia. But a more immediate problem was a white man who had stolen a tribal chief's woman. And if a riot would occur in one of the Allied work camps, it would disrupt transportation essential to the Northern Territory and the war effort. There, in that dugout, as I looked at a map of Australia, to get their location, I was struck by the similarities of our two countries.

If a map of the United States were superimposed onto the Australian continent — the land down under the equator — the two countries would appear to be identical geographically. The four corners match each other exactly: Melbourne with Miami Beach; Townsville with Boston; Darwin with Seattle; and Perth with San Diego, both having large naval bases. Only the jagged top end of Australia differs from the northern straight edge of the United States.

Both countries were settled by immigrants from Great Britain and both spoke a common language. Their eastern coastlines were the first areas to be developed as new settlers arrived on their respective shores. Though coming from different backgrounds and migrating for different reasons, our settlers' lifestyles grew along similar lines.

Australia's love of horse racing and draft beer gave it an aura of the much earlier "Gay '90s" era in the United States. Now war had brought our two countries together in the Northern Territory of Australia.

As a member of the United States Armed Forces in Australia, USAFIA, I was an intruder in the land of these primitive people. Alone in the dark radio station, my thoughts drifted back to the life I had lived on a 160-acre farm back in the United States, before my enlistment into the Regular Army at Fort Leavenworth, Kansas, some 18 months earlier. I began to review the circumstances that led to my becoming a soldier and my being stationed to this awesome "Land Down Under." I was committed to stopping the Japanese threat to Australia and freedom-loving people around the world.

Born on a farm in the rolling hills west of the Missouri River in Atchison County, Kansas, I grew up wearing bib overalls, the eighth of nine children. My parents were first-generation Americans of immigrant parentage. I was an American. I lived by faith in the Son of God. I was an instrument of His peace.

My mother, "Maggie" Scott, and her five brothers and five sisters were reared near the Iowa Sac and Fox Indian reservation in southeastern Nebraska. In fact, Mom was traded to a Sioux squaw for an Indian pony when she was a little blond toddler playing at Grandpa Scott's watering tank near their home in Preston. Leading a spotted pony, an Indian squaw approached Grandma Scott, talking and pointing to little blond Maggie. Grandma Julia didn't understand the Sioux language and just nodded her head. The Indian thought a trade had been made, and Grandma soon noticed her little girl was gone, but there was an extra pony at the tank. Grandpa Scott had to do some fast riding to get Mom back.

My Dad's father emigrated to the United States in an unusual way. In 1858, as a lad of 16, working at an English seaport, Grandpa Charles Wyatt crawled into a barrel and was rolled aboard a ship bound for the

United States. He joined a wagon train in Lancaster County, Pennsylvania, that was going West and eventually became a farm hand near Falls City, Nebraska. My dad, Joseph Wyatt, courted my mother in horse-and-buggy days when funerals, weddings, and church socials were the main events in young people's lives.

During my grade school days I walked from our farm, a mile east of Effingham, Kansas, to St. Ann's Church in town, to serve the priest at Mass each morning during summer vacations. I learned about freedom and democracy from my six sisters and brother. Though I didn't get to vote on some of their programs then, such as who cleaned the chicken house or filled the washtubs each Monday morning, the 1920s and 1930s were the happiest, most carefree, days of my life. I fondly remember one spring morning after a rain as my shepherd dog and I drove the cows in to be milked, we crossed the ruts in our Bluegrass pasture made by pioneer wagons.

During my grade school years I rode a horse to school. An active student, I won athletic letters in all sports and had leading roles in several operettas at our county-community high school before graduating with the class of 1938. My favorite place was the school library where the world was at my beck and call. There I could study events outside the boundaries of our farm fence lines. Life was worth living and freedom was taken for granted and just accepted.

Working with my parents and siblings on the farm, I learned family values and to accept responsibility for my own actions. I was free to think, to question, and to act on my own because my family believed in the constitutional government our founders had established based on law and a Bill of Rights for all to live by.

I helped my parents survive the Great Depression and hard times of the "Dirty '30s" when drought and dust storms enveloped the Great Plains states. Chickens went to roost at 3 o'clock some afternoons due to clouds of thick dust that blackened the entire western horizon. And some of our horses died of fistula and sleeping sickness.

Mom made meals of wheat cracked by a meat grinder then sweetened with molasses and roasted in the oven of our woodburning stove. We had our cows for milk, and Dad butchered cattle and hogs for our meat. We ate a lot of chicken soup, scrawny potatoes, and vegetables from a drouthy garden. We lived off the land and bought only our coffee, sugar, salt, and flour in town. Mom bought flour in 100-pound sacks, from which she

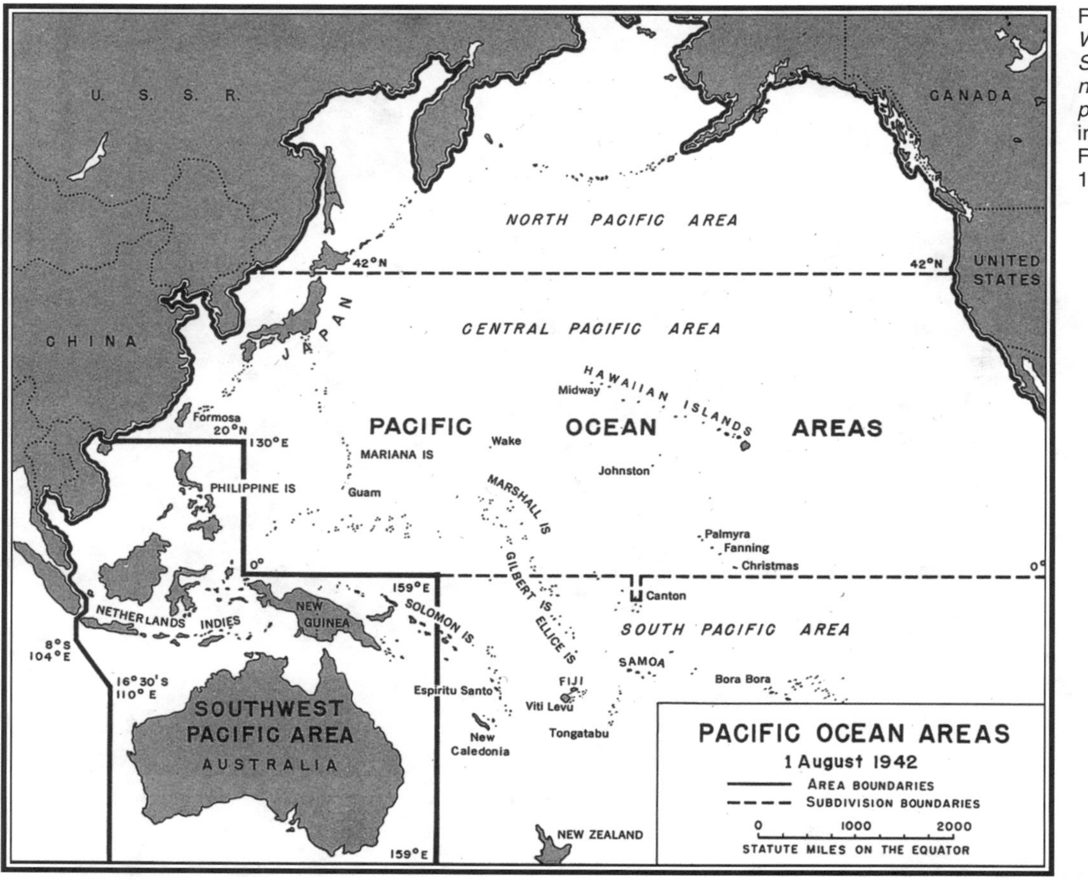

From *United States Army in World War II, The Technical Services: The Corps of Engineers: The War Against Japan*, by Karl C. Dodd (Washington, D.C.: Office of Air Force History, U.S. Army, 1966), 129.

The Wyatt farm home when the author left in September 1941.
Ray Wyatt photo

The Atchison County Community High School Big Six Conference Champions, 1938. Front, l to r: Al Becker, Tom Yazel, D. Cooper, D. Burns, J. Thorne, J. Powell, and C. Foster; rear, l to r: Fritz Scott, Ray Wyatt, Mike Strine, and Glen Higley.

Shortly after this picture was taken of the author's mother and an orphaned lamb, he walked down the farm lane to the highway to Fort Leavenworth and enlisted in the Regular Army, on September 9, 1941.
Ray Wyatt photo

made dresses for my sisters. Eight O'Clock coffee came in a *bean* and was put through a grinder in the store. What wonderful odors came from that old country store!

Those were the days when no one in our family went to the doctor unless there was a broken bone or severe injury. Dad would say, "If you go to see the doctor, you better damn well be sick!" I didn't go to a hospital until I was in the Service.

We were poor, but didn't know it. In fact, the farming operation was a losing proposition and only the cream check from the dairy cows and Mom's egg check from her old hens kept us from starving.

My older brother, Joe, had joined the Civilian Conservation Corps (CCC) in 1933 at a camp near Hiawatha, Kansas. With other young men, he helped build earthen dams and east-west windbreaks called shelter belts across the state. His pay was $30 per month, of which $25 was sent home to Mom and Dad. The bank foreclosed on our farm in 1934 when I was 14, and we moved to other farms to stay alive. Grasshoppers wiped out our corn crops and chinch bugs took the wheat during those drought years. But those were God-fearing, character-building experiences, as well as a time of desperation for man and beast.

World events were low priority to this country boy in middle America. News of farm events and local weather reports were our immediate concern. Harvesting the corn crop and "puttin' up" the hay were more important on our quiet eastern Kansas farm. We seldom listened to our battery-operated radio because Mom wanted to save the "juice" for Fibber McGee and Molly, or George Burns and Gracie Allen. Our only newspaper was the weekly *Effingham New Leaf.*

My world was the farm, my church, and high school sports. And because of Mom's restrictions on the radio, I didn't take the war raging in Europe seriously. The U.S. economy in 1940 was just beginning to recover and I was restless to become somebody other than a farmer.

Overseas, Germany had invaded Poland in September 1939 and in the ensuing years conquered nearly all of Europe. Fearing we would become involved, the United States began gearing up for war production. Under the Lend-Lease Act passed in March 1941, President Franklin D. Roosevelt declared America "the arsenal of democracy" for all freedom-loving countries around the world. It seemed to me that put us in the war.

At the time of these world events I attended St. Benedict's College in Atchison, Kansas, under a football scholarship, and my sisters and brother pursued their own careers. All of us were within a day's journey of home. I did not want to spend my life in the fields of Kansas, but I had no skills worthy of employment in industry.

During the summer of 1940, the war in Europe accelerated and on September 16th the U.S. Congress passed the Selective Training and Service Act — the Draft — calling up all men age 21 through 35. Men from Atchison County and across America became "Draftees," with a number for the "call up" or lottery. I would not be of Draft age until August 1941.

In March 1941 I enrolled in a correspondence course offered by TWA, Transcontinental and Western Airlines, based in Kansas City. I wanted to be a radio operator on a major airline and fly in a DC-3, the new workhorse of the commercial airlines. The course consisted of several texts on airline operations and included a small windup tape recorder and spools of half-inch ticker tape with the Morse Code punched onto it. Airline radio operators had to know the International Morse Code, and thus, in my bedroom on the second floor of our Kansas farm home, I learned to receive the code through earphones and to send with a telegrapher's hand key.

When I turned 21, on August 6, 1941, the war in Europe was nearly two years old. Germany had attacked Russia and had overrun most of her European neighbors. During this time the Japanese empire was building a huge military power in the South Pacific and Southeast Asia and had one of the largest naval forces in the world. It became an obvious threat to the Philippine Islands, a commonwealth of the United States, and to all of the oil and mineral rich islands in the South Seas.

Even quiet farm life was threatened. Men in the 137th Infantry Regiment, Kansas National Guard, from Atchison County were on maneuvers in Louisiana. These were the renowned prewar "Louisiana maneuvers," the first time since World War I that major forces had been so engaged. Rumors circulated that the Guards were an unhappy lot — typical of the isolationist Americans of the time — and were chanting, "OHIO . . . Over the Hill in October!" That meant desertion — going AWOL. Letters sent home indicated the men were required to play war games, using wooden guns to attack trucks marked "TANK" in order to simulate battle conditions. Yet, at the same time, American guns and ammunition were being shipped overseas to England and Russia.

A feeling of gloom and doubt permeated every township in our county. Men were being called "Draft dodgers" if they sought ways to be reclassified by their county Draft board. Mothers encouraged their sons to get married and start a family in order to avoid the Draft, and some farm boys were reported to be jumping off tall hog sheds to flatten their feet. But I didn't want any part of flat feet, or marriage!

One month after my 21st birthday, I decided to enlist, not so much for patriotic reasons but to be able to select the branch of Service I wanted. It looked like the U.S. soon would be involved in the war in Europe, which could go on for several years.

Early on the morning of September 9th I walked down our long lane and thumbed a ride to Fort Leavenworth with "Peck" Benjamin, a local plumber. I did not realize the severity of the international gang war that was about to envelop the United States and the world, or the impact it would have on my personal life.

Before arriving at the Fort I decided that I didn't want to be a foot soldier or an artilleryman. On my enlistment papers I was classified as a farm equipment operator. And since I could send and receive the International Morse Code at eight to ten words per minute, I asked the recruiting officer for the Army Signal Corps. He said he would contact them to see if there was an opening. After that I was issued "Dog Tags," two metal tags on which were imprinted the number 17020080, the letter C (for Catholic), and the letter O (for my blood type). The tags were on a chain, which I was ordered to put around my neck and never take off, even in the shower. These tags contained information for treatment in case of injury or hospitalization.

After a miserable week of shots and KP — Kitchen Police — peeling potatoes, sweeping and scrubbing floors, and cleaning tables to look busy, I was told that a vacancy existed in the 15th Battalion, 997th Signal Service Company, at Fort Monmouth, New Jersey. I accepted and immediately called my dad and mom back on the farm.

On the next Sunday afternoon, my parents came to see and support me with their love and concerns. My mother was upset, not from bidding me Godspeed but from my dad having taken the wrong turn to get to the Fort. The entrance to the federal penitentiary can be mistaken for the gate to Fort Leavenworth and Dad, not familiar with those different entrances, took the first one to the "Big House." Then, because of a hearing problem, Dad didn't respond to the prison guard's command to halt and be recognized. Visitors had to have a definite reason for entering a federal penitentiary. The alternative could result in being shot. Dad drove right up to the steps leading to the two big doors into the prison and stepped out of the car. He was intent on seeing his son in the U.S. Army. The guard again ordered him to halt, and leveled a gun at his back. Mom could hear and see what was going on, but Dad kept right on going up the steps! Mom had to take action. When she yelled at him in a familiar voice, he turned and saw guards pointing guns at his chest. He corrected his course post haste. Later he told me he swallowed his "chaw of tobaccer" right there!

When the time arrived for me to leave Fort Leavenworth, I was really excited in anticipation of seeing New York and the East Coast states. Dressed in new Army suntans and carrying a suitcase full of civilian clothes, I boarded the Santa Fe Super Chief at Union Station in Kansas City on September 16, 1941, a memorable day in my life. I was on my way to new adventures. I was a soldier in the Regular Army of the United States of America and a Private, no less. (It's impossible to be less in the Army!)

But it was nice! I had never been east of the Kansas border before. Now I was in a Pullman sleeping-car and looking out across the Missouri countryside, like a big dog in the back of a pickup. I had dinner in a diner and "nothing could be finer." That night I slept in the upper berth of a fast-moving, smooth-riding train across Illinois. When I awoke the next morning and looked out the window, I saw unbelievable miles and miles of corn fields with beautiful farmsteads stretching across the horizon. I marveled that the United States was so big!

At Fort Wayne, Indiana, I saw the most automobiles I had ever seen at one time in one place, in an employee parking lot. There must have been more than a hundred of them there behind an industrial building. That night I saw the Pennsylvania steel mills and smelters going full blast in the big yards as the train pulled through the cities. What a wonder world our America was to this farm boy!

Upon arrival at Fort Monmouth, about 50 miles south of Staten Island as the crow flies, I reported to the Headquarters of the 15th Signal Corps Battalion barracks. After being issued new ODs, olive-drab clothing for winter wear, I was assigned a bunk on the third floor of a building that would hold a company of men, or a lot of hay. I'd never slept that high off the ground before. I soon learned I was the only Westerner among recruits mostly from East Coast states.

My first morning in the big toilet on the third floor of Headquarters barracks was a revelation to me. Ten to twenty men wrapped in towels or just wearing shorts stood shaving in front of a long row of basins and mirrors — nothing unusual, except that I had never smelled so many wonderful shaving lotions before in my life. It was a far cry from our old outhouse back on the farm! Here the crappers flushed with running water. What would they think of next?

During the following weeks in basic training I worked at becoming a soldier by familiarizing myself with Army drills and regulations. I learned to "fall out" for reveille, "fall in" for drill, and how and whom to salute. It took a while to learn what the different stripes meant and who was a "looie" and who was a "kernel." I soon caught on by watching for officers while I policed the area for cigarette butts and bits of trash. I had entered the military world!

During peacetime, soldiers got weekend passes and wore civilian clothes when off duty. In a matter of weeks I had been to New York City several times, by way of the Lincoln Tunnel, and was getting used to the fall weather along the Atlantic Coast. One of my first assignments was to accompany a six-wheeled truck full of laundry to a cleaning establishment near the New York City harbor. We drove the trucks onto a ferry and crossed over to Staten Island. As I looked out across the water, I saw the immense skyline of New York City, and the Statue of Liberty. What a sight! How did they get that much steel and stone onto one place? Everybody had a radio. The announcers talked about "dem Dodgers" and "da Yankees." I attended a big concert in Madison Square Garden and visited with a soldier buddy's family in Queens where I went to a Sunday Mass.

One Saturday morning after emerging from the Lincoln Tunnel, we were stopped by an oncoming fire engine with red lights flashing. In the open cab of the truck was the bareheaded mayor of New York City, Fiorello LaGuardia. It was reported that he was giving New Yorkers an example of what to do to support the city in the event of an air raid. The East Coast was practicing alerts because of the intensity of the war in Europe and reports of U.S. ships being sunk along the Atlantic Coast.

I was fascinated by 42nd Street, Times Square, and the tall buildings. I and another GI rode to the top of the Empire State Building in an elevator, taking some 90 floors before the first stop. On reaching the top and looking down at the street below, I felt a sudden urge to jump over the edge. A Piper Cub flew by almost level with us. And then an unforgettable sight unfolded. All the lights along the Great White Way came on at once as the sun's last rays tinted the western horizon. It was awesome! That memory has lasted through some 50 years.

On another evening, I went to the new Stage Door Canteen USO off 42nd Street, where I talked to Katharine Cornell, the actress. I finished that evening by seeing the Ice Capades and Radio City Music Hall in Rockefeller Center.

Reveille was at 6:00 a.m. each morning in front of the Battalion barracks. The weather by that time was below freezing at night, and each day it became harder and harder to "fall in" properly dressed and wait for the ranks to fill. The scene at reveille one particularly cold Monday morning was something to write home about. Nearly half the third floor was missing, and many who fell in were wearing only long underwear and shirts. One disheveled soldier was barefooted and wearing an overcoat over his shorts and T-shirt. Another was barely able to stand in unlaced boots, while his shorts were partially tucked into open-fly pants. Like the words in a song, "I don't want no more of Army life. Hey! Man, I want to go home," military life for recruits was in a laid-back mode in the fall of 1941, before Pearl Harbor.

That was about to change.

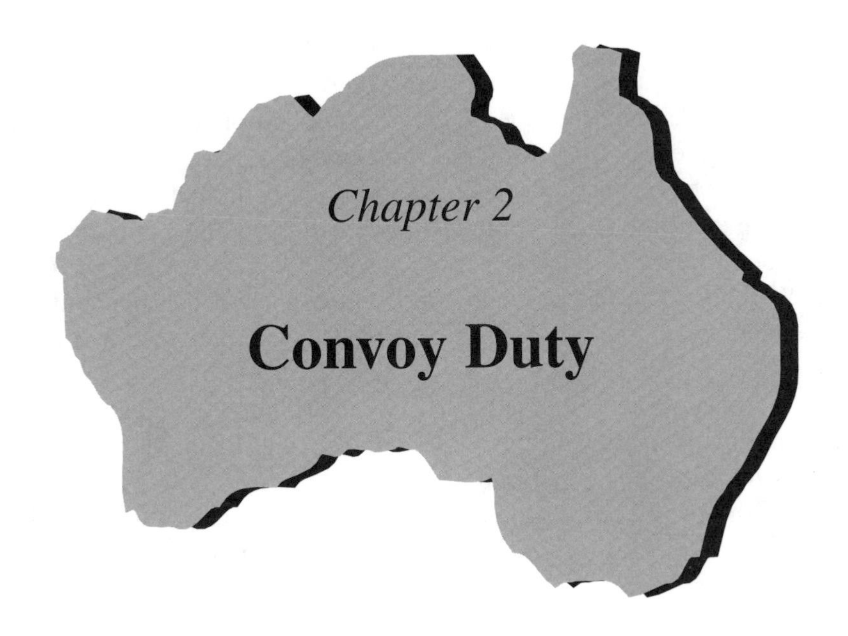

Chapter 2

Convoy Duty

LIFE IN THE ARMY for farm boys accustomed to getting up at daybreak and walking a mile to bring in the cows and horses would be called a "pudd" today. Army life was easy compared to working from sunup to sundown all summer long and walking several miles a day behind a plow or hay wagon.

My favorite exercise at Fort Monmouth was close-order drills. I liked the camaraderie of a big group of us swinging along and responding to the Drill Sergeant's commands. I had only one day-long march and it was easy — probably less than 10 miles there in New Jersey. The favorite trick of our Drill Instructor was to give a "To the rear, harch" command to see if everyone was listening. Guys crashing into each other told him we were not.

I got "gigged" once and had to do KP for a week. During my first company inspection, as we stood in front of the review stand at the parade ground west of our barracks, a high-ranking officer walked up and down our columns checking our dress and shoe shine and hair-cut. Before the parade, we had been warned by the First Sergeant to shine, wear a clean tie, and stand erect with our chest out. I was sure I had done all those things when the officers stopped in front of me and pointed to my waistline. *My God! What did I do wrong?*

I had my belt on the wrong way. It took an Army inspection to learn that men wore their belt buckle on the left side with the tongue pointing left. I found out a long time later that women's belts were worn just the opposite. Well, after all, farmers wore bib overalls most of the time and used suspenders for church services or dress; belts were not often part of our attire.

One aspect of my first month's training that I didn't anticipate were the sessions involving bayonet practice. I didn't like being shown how to attack and thrust a bayonet into a swinging dummy who represented the enemy. And because of a shortage of rifles, we were taught to fire a blue-steel Colt .45 on the firing range. So I didn't have an opportunity to earn a marksman's medal.

Two recruits on the third floor of our barracks were noticed by everyone. One was a lean, quiet fellow of medium build with a sharp ridged nose on his narrow face. He didn't enter into conversations unless invited. He said he was from Tennessee and was nicknamed "Hawkeye." One night, watching him and a guy from Arkansas play pool in the company basement, I realized why he had the name. When he leaned over and eyed the ball on the end of the cue stick, he absolutely resembled a hawk. He was hard to communicate with, and I wondered why he was in the Signal Corps, whose purpose was communication!

The other guy could justifiably be called a character. One night while we sat on the third-floor balcony of Headquarters barracks he told me he was from West Virginia and had been sent to Fort Monmouth to learn communication skills for his outfit, the artillery. He proudly said he was a mule-skinner. He worked with mules all day, pulling two-wheeled cannons and supply wagons through mountainous terrain somewhere in the Allegheny Mountains. With his beady black eyes between a large Roman nose and protruding teeth in his receding chin, he looked like a mule. His nickname was even "Muley," and he loved it. He admitted he liked mules better than he did most humans and enjoyed the interaction with the animals while grooming and taking care of them.

During my first two months in basic training, Muley and I did a lot of time together "policing" cigarette butts around the barracks and parade ground. He was not very talkative, and tended to be shy. In a crowd, he usually could be found slouched over at the edge of the group of GIs. He moved about deliberate and slow. He was something to watch.

Muley and I loved to police butts, just to see who could find the longest. As a poor farm boy, my first cigarette was a roll-your-own kind. I remember trying to roll one using flimsy cigarette paper and lumpy, moist *Prince Albert* tobacco in a can. *Bull Durham* was best for rolling your own; the papers came with the bag. With practice and holding still, you could make a neat, smooth cigarette with *Bull Durham* nearly every time. My brother's crowd, in the 1930s, thought it was smart to roll your own. Sometimes they were not as "firm and fully packed," as they thought they were, and the makin's tumbled out the lighted end of the thing, like small meteors. They could have burned the barn down.

But at Fort Monmouth in 1941, I didn't see any roll-your-own butts. They were mostly *Lucky Strikes*, *Camels*, and *Chesterfields*. Once in awhile we found a new kind, called *Menthol* or *Kool*. Muley was very selective. He picked up only those more than an inch and a half long with no lip stains. He stuck them in his left shirt pocket. I watched other guys who were right-handed, too, and their cigarettes were in their left front pocket and they drew their butts out with their right forefinger. They kept their lighter in their right pocket. Some guys had brown stains on the inside of the two forefingers of their left hand where they held the "fag" while engaged in conversation. You could tell how important a guy was by the way he handled his cigarette.

Well, so it was with Muley. He said that when he went into the service he brought his own cigarette papers and *Bull Durham*. When I joined up, I liked *Lucky Strikes*. I was never any good at rolling cigarettes. My uncle back home could roll them with one hand and strike a kitchen match with his thumbnail. He was good. He could roll a cigarette with his left finger and thumb so easily that people stopped to watch.

At Fort Monmouth in the fall of 1941, Muley and I found all manufactured cigarette butts. Doesn't that tell you how affluent American men were? At the end of a butt-hunting day we smelled like tobacco smoke, from the collection in our left shirt pockets. But, what the hell. We weren't trying to date girls or bucking for Sergeant stripes. I often wonder what happened to Muley — a real, genuine mule-skinner from the mountains of West Virginia and a real *Bull Durham* man.

The barracks the author lived in while attending the 1st Signal Company, 15th Battalion, Signal Corps School, at Fort Monmouth, New Jersey, before going overseas in April 1942.

One month after arriving at Fort Monmouth I was on the operating table at the base hospital having my appendix removed. Some of that was brought on by the rich food and beer I had consumed while on weekend passes to New York City. The operation was successful. My third oldest sister, a nurse in a Kansas City hospital, told me to have a spinal block. I didn't know what that meant, but it hastened my recovery. I watched the operation and talked to a gray-haired doctor while he hooked the stitches in sewing up the incision. When I was taken into the recovery room, patients around me reeked of ether and vomited, sometimes bursting their stitches. Fortunately, I didn't have a problem and was back in my barracks in three or four days on limited duty.

One crisp November night in a cafe diner in Oceanside, I had coffee with the company First Sergeant. Knowing of my operation and duty status, he asked me if I would like to go on convoy duty. He explained that it would entail riding trains with three other soldiers as armed guards of Signal Corps equipment being shipped to the West Coast. I would have to carry a gun and jump off to guard the equipment each time the train stopped, in all kinds of weather. He offered me a choice of going to Florida or a trip to the Presidio of San Francisco, in California. I chose California, which would take 12 days round-trip.

U.S. Army Signal Corps Privates Ray Wyatt (l) and Paul Fredericks wearing winter uniforms, September 1941, at Fort Monmouth, New Jersey. Paul had played second trumpet in the Alvino Rey Orchestra before entering the service. *Ray Wyatt photo*

Above and opposite: Part of the 15th Signal Service Regiment, Fort Monmouth, New Jersey, October 9, 1941. Private Wyatt is fifth from left in the second row.

On the appointed day, three other GIs and I reported to the Supply Room, where I was issued a U.S. Cavalry pistol with a seven-inch barrel, and seven rounds of ammunition.

"You mean I gotta carry that thing?"

The Corporal growled back, "You can take it or shove it. Just sign here that I gave it to you."

A First Lieutenant had been assigned to accompany us. Our orders were to allow no one to touch the equipment loaded on two railroad flatcars now waiting on a siding near Redbank, New Jersey.

When we arrived at the freight yards, a caboose, our living quarters for the trip, was being attached to the flatcars, at the end of the train. We became acquainted with the train's flagman who operated from another caboose at the front of our equipment.

Our train was made up of a long line of cars and powered by a beautiful big steam engine, the ingenious invention of some very enterprising individuals of the early 1800s. It was hard to imagine the manufacturing of such an immense piece of equipment powered by steam and controlled from a little overhead cab back of the big boilers. The train crew con-

sisted of an engineer, a fireman, a head brakeman, and a rear conductor or flagman.

As the other soldiers and I settled onto our bunks in our caboose, I thought of the wonderful days back home when I had watched black smoke drift slowly over our farm from passing trains. We lived just a half mile south of the Missouri Pacific tracks that passed through Effingham. I was amazed by the size of the drive wheels and by the fact that only a very small surface of those wheels was in contact with the rails. As a young boy I had seen an engineer spin those big wheels by giving them too much power at once.

I loved the smells of steam engines and watching the smoke billow from the stack while a train was stopped at a station. I recalled that at wheat-threshing time on the farm, I ran down the road to meet the crew driving the steam engine that pulled the threshing machine up the road to our farm lane. Mr. Congrove, our local threshing machine operator, allowed me to ride on the engine's water tank when he turned into our place the day they threshed our grain.

While I was reminiscing, our train slowly left the station at Redbank. Our convoy duties had begun.

Pulling out of Redbank, our trip began on the Nickel Plate railroad owned by New York Central Lines. It operated between New York and Chicago. Nickel had been incorporated into the rails to test the impact of the wheels on the rails, as compared to regular iron rails. In a matter of a few hours we were moving through lush Pennsylvania countryside. As a kid, I often had imagined what it would be like to be an engineer, or even a hobo "ridin' the rails." Now here I was, a U.S. soldier, totin' a big gun and seeing America the best way — from the caboose of a train. This was an exciting way to go.

Our train slowed as we entered each town. I usually took a position in the cupola of our caboose so that I could hang my arm out the window and wave at kids who were always happy to see a train. Each time we came to a major city, we four soldiers, following the flagman's signal, jumped off and took positions alongside our load. At a signal from the engineer — a series of toots — we loaded back on our caboose as the train moved on again.

Early in the morning of a wintery day, we pulled into the big railyards of Chicago on a siding near Lake Michigan. A cold mist was swirling off the lake, forming ice on trees and buildings as we walked our patrol. I had never been so cold, not even in windy Kansas. The cold and humidity soon became unbearable and forced us to seek the shelter of the caboose. When we finally chugged out of Chicago, I was glad to see the dawn and feel the warm sunshine as we moved across northern Illinois.

Our route took us straight west. We passed through western Nebraska at night and the next morning found ourselves in Cheyenne, Wyoming. On that cold daybreak, as we stood beside our equipment in the Cheyenne railyards, a dozen U.S. Cavalrymen rode by on horseback. When they saw us, they pointed to our big guns hanging cowboy style on our legs and burst into laughter, yelling, "Where did you get those guns?"

We were toting their usual Cavalry weapons, while they were wearing spiffy blue-steel snubnosed .45s. We yelled back, "This is the Army. You take what you're issued!"

Moving on, later that day we passed Sparks, Nevada, and began the climb into the Sierra Nevada Mountains of California, coming upon numerous snowsheds as we progressed. Big snow plows belched glistening plumes of white powder from the railroad right-of-way. We spent most of the day making our way slowly through the snowsheds of the Sierras and down into the San Joaquin Valley of California.

On the afternoon of the fifth day, we delivered our equipment and man-

The two-storied building on the right was the overseas barracks where Signal detachments were readied for shipment in April 1942. *Ray Wyatt photo*

ifest to the Presidio of San Francisco. There I saw the Golden Gate Bridge for the first time. Who could fail to be impressed by that magnificent structure arching over the blue waters of San Francisco Bay in the bright sunlight?

After a big dinner in the Presidio mess hall, our Lieutenant took us to a downtown hotel where he dismissed us with an admonition not to return to Fort Monmouth before our twelfth day. An early return meant turning in our unused pay and confusing the paymaster. The Lieutenant told us we could stay in the hotel in San Francisco — or take off for Timbuktu. With a whole extra day to make it back to the Fort, I chose to catch a train to Kansas that afternoon, because it was a chance to see my parents on the way. I rode the luxurious Santa Fe Super Chief to Omaha where I took the Missouri Pacific to Atchison, and home. I visited with my parents, helping Dad with chores. He was 65, and arthritis was beginning to invade his hands. He didn't understand why I had to go into the Service. And I didn't realize at the time that it would be the last time I was to see him.

I caught a train to Omaha and arrived back in New Jersey at Fort Monmouth on time. At Battalion Headquarters, the First Sergeant greeted me with a smile and asked, "Do you wanna go again?"

I nodded and said, "Sure."

On a cold Monday morning late in November, three other soldiers and I were railside at Redbank station ready again to embark on "Frontier Americana." This time a Captain was our leader. He was an older man, a Signal Corps career officer eager to get away from a desk job. The load was the same, but the trip took a different route across the country. We were using "Red Ball Freight," a term used by the railroads to indicate special treatment, or top priority. Even passenger trains were sidetracked for Red Ball Freight.

On the first leg of our journey, our train stopped in Altoona, Pennsylvania, at night. The flagman told us we would be in the yards for several hours. He asked if any of us would like to watch them "humping cars." I eagerly volunteered. So I rode with him to the top of a hill in the big yards at the edge of the city. From a small tower I watched a short, stubby yard engine pull a freight car from the train and hump it to the top of the hill where the operator in the tower switched it a track down the other side of the hill to its proper destination. Hence the term "humping." It was an ingenious arrangement.

As we left Altoona the next morning I saw my first "hobo jungle," a gathering place in the thickets and ditches along the tracks where vagrants and hobos built fires and set up stoves and other amenities for survival. These were permanent locations where vagabonds could find food and protection with their own kind. They were not really "jungles" but more like hobo motels.

Chicago was not as cold or windy this time, and we traveled in a newly painted Santa Fe caboose for the rest of the trip. What a good deal that was. The caboose had neat bunks and upholstered chairs that swiveled in a complete circle. It also had a small, wood-burning stove near the center of the bunk area. It still smelled of new paint. One night as the Captain and I sat in the cupola of the train's caboose, rolling along west of St. Louis, we saw large cakes of ice floating in the moonlit stream of the Missouri River. It was a beautiful and relaxing moment.

The next night our slow-moving train ran into a fierce blizzard some 200 miles west of Kansas City near Great Bend, Kansas. Snow blowing under the rear door began to drift into the middle of our caboose. We were miserable, and the cold began to numb our fingers. The Captain didn't know what to do for warmth, so the guys wrapped themselves in every blanket and coat available. When the engineer stopped the engine in front of the Great Bend station, I jumped from the caboose and ran along the side of the train and into the building. The trainmen gathered by a large round, white-hot stove made room for me. When the engineer indicated he was ready to move out, we all headed back to our posts. But nothing happened. The train didn't move. Believe it or not, the steam engine had frozen up. A small petcock on a cylinder that fed steam to the bigger cylinders running the big drive wheels was exposed to the wind and cold while the train idled at the station. The little petcock froze, preventing the steam from getting to the big cylinders. A blow torch and a hot poker solved the problem.

When I got back to our caboose, snow had drifted into the center of the bunk area. Everyone was huddled on the bunks, immobile. No one could talk. It was a beastly cold death ward as the train lumbered westward into the night.

At dawn, when the train stopped at the edge of a western Kansas town, I jumped out and gathered some boards and chunks of coal that had fallen out of coal bins of previous trains. Using paper and shavings, I started a fire in the small stove in the center of the caboose. In due time, I had a good blaze going and we began shedding blankets. Not one of those soldiers knew how to start a fire. The Captain credited me with saving our lives, and I credited myself as lucky to have been born a Kansas farm boy!

The Santa Fe route took us through Flagstaff, Arizona, where one snowy afternoon my trip nearly ended. Crewmen of the old steam trains used a series of toots to signal what was happening. Four toots by the engineer told the conductor the train would move forward; three toots meant he was going to back the train; two toots was a "Yes" to the flagman; and one long toot meant, "We're moving out." The flagman would swing his lantern back and forth to reply.

When our train stopped on a slight decline on the west side of Flagstaff, I thought I knew the signals. But, somehow I missed the single toot, and I was at the farthest point on my patrol. When the train began to move I was nearly 50 yards ahead of the rear caboose and the train was really rolling. My only hope was to catch hold of the grab bar on its side as it passed, and hang on, or risk being stranded in Flagstaff. The train was doing about 10 mph when the caboose got to me. I planted my right foot on the bottom step of the platform and grabbed for the sidebar. I ended up sprawled on my stomach across the rear deck, with my head protruding over the side. My shins were sore for a week! I paid more attention to the toots after that.

At Indio, California, the biggest steam engines manufactured were put on the front and rear of our train. They were 4664s: four small wheels under the front trucks, six big driver wheels, then six more big drivers and four small wheels under the rear trucks. They resembled two regular engines welded back to back with locomotion in either direction. These big engines were used to push freight trains up the long grade west of Palm Springs through Cabazon Pass in the San Bernardino Mountains. The next day, we were in the San Joaquin Valley and delivered the signal equipment to the Presidio of Monterey.

Before making these trips I wondered why soldiers needed to carry guns and live ammunition on United States railroads. By the time the trips were over, I realized how many times strange-looking men had approached us in the railroad yards and asked questions pertaining to our load. They wanted information on the contents of the flatcars, the origin of the shipment, and where it was going . . . valuable information to saboteurs. Even away from the yards, the equipment was not safe. In railyards of nearly every city, suspicious-looking characters pressed us for answers as to what we were hauling. Our answer was always the same: "Eggs."

One evening as we began a slow crawl west out of Indio, California, a scruffy-looking fellow jumped from behind a bush and ran alongside our equipment. When he threw his satchel over into our load and started to climb aboard, the soldier on that side of the caboose took a shot at him. He fell away from the train, pulling his satchel with him. No telling what was in that satchel. The soldier paid the Captain $1.05 — five cents for the bullet and $1.00 to keep him out of civil courts.

After delivering our manifest and load to Army officials at the Presidio at Monterey, we caught a passenger train back to Fort Monmouth, arriving there on December 6th. My contribution to the security of the United States had been worthwhile. I felt important, and I loved riding trains.

Back at the barracks on Sunday afternoon, December 7th, I went to see a movie at the post theater. Believe it or not, the movie was about Sergeant York who had captured more than a hundred German soldiers by himself during World War I. When I walked out of that theater, I was ready to fight the enemy! Little did I know I would soon have the chance. Everywhere in the barracks radios were blasting a report of the Japanese attack on Pearl Harbor.

The next day, December 8, 1941, President Roosevelt declared war on Japan — a day that would "live in infamy." We were at war. Life in America would never again be the same.

Chapter 3

Signal Corps School

ONE OF THE OLDEST forms of communication is the smoke signal. On March 11, 1942, when General Douglas MacArthur, his family, and staff escaped from Corregidor to Mindanao, Philippine Islands, on the motor torpedo boat *PT-41*, the Japanese lit signal fires along the island shorelines. It was a crude and ineffective means of communication because the General's party made it to safety in Darwin, Australia, undetected and unaffected.

My introduction to the world of communications had begun with the old wooden telephone with the long mouthpiece and crank-type ringer. It hung on the dining room wall of our farm home. Everyone on our "party line" had a different combination of long and short rings to identify their number. You could tell who was being called by listening to the different rings. Mom said it was "bad manners" to listen in on the neighbor's calls but temptation often overruled, especially if one of the neighbor girls was a "hot number." When I walked along our township road as a barefoot boy, I couldn't imagine that those wires strung along on the poles past our house carried voices.

One summer a neighbor and I tried to develop our own telephone system. We rigged up two Pork and Bean cans with 100 yards of telephone wire we found laying on the ground along the township road beyond our pasture fence. With a pair of pliers, we fastened the ends of the telephone wire into each can and then yelled into the open ends of the cans as we stood some hundred yards apart. It didn't work, but our inventive urge was sparked for future reference.

My inventive curiosity was further heightened each time I walked past the Missouri Pacific railroad station in Effingham. I could hear the telegrapher's handkey as he sent messages down a wire to the next station in Atchison, on the banks of the Missouri River, 17 miles away. His wire was energized by a battery, or an electric current, and was called continuous wave (CW) transmission. Code transmission is the result of the carrier wave being interrupted by an operator holding the key down, or breaking the circuit with short and long intervals, corresponding to the dots and dashes representing the letters of the alphabet. Wireless transmission was created by an electrically powered transmitter emitting electromagnetic waves that radiated through the air as carrier waves on which were modulated impulses. These waves acted as a carrier for both code and voice communication. Anyone with a receiver tuned to those transmitted frequencies could pick them up.

I was fascinated by the world of communication that resulted from the discovery of electromagnetism. And at Fort Monmouth, I was given the opportunity to learn more of this operation at one of the nation's top communication schools.

Fort Monmouth was one of four major Signal Corps posts offering training for officers and enlisted men before World War II. Other Signal Corps training camps included the Presidio of Monterey, California, Leon Springs, Texas, and Fort Leavenworth, Kansas.

Fort Monmouth began in June 1917 as Camp Little Silver on Governor's Island, New York, with 25 officers and 451 enlisted men. Within three months it was renamed Camp Alfred Vail. Vail was an associate of Samuel Morse, inventor of the telegraph and contributor to wire communications. By the end of 1917, 2,416 enlisted men and 448 officers were processed at Camp Vail.

America's first military pilots and their flying machines had been originally grouped, August 1, 1907, as an aeronautical division of the Signal Corps. From July 18, 1914, through May 20, 1928, they were simply called the Air Corps. Subsequently, beginning June 20, 1941, and through World War II, everyone knew them as the Army Air Forces. Since September 18, 1947, they have been the United States Air Force, now independent of other military Services.

The need to train specialists in *wireless* communication for tank and aerial warfare was evident in European battle conditions during World War I and resulted in the development of new laboratories for air combat units of the Army now at Fort Monmouth. Twenty light aircraft were used for testing new inventions, particularly direction-finding by radio. Late in 1917, four hangars and two airfields were built at the Fort to accommodate the planes used for the experiments. Because radio transmission was not always effective during electrical storms, other types of communications — like pigeons — were included in the studies.

Carrier pigeons proved to be useful in World War I. Support for the program was generated by a pigeon named *Bon Ami*, who saved the day by flying wounded through the German lines during the battle of the Black Forest in the Argonne Sector. My uncle was killed in that battle on the last day before the signing of the Armistice at 11:00 a.m., on the eleventh day, of the eleventh month of 1918. Birds at Fort Monmouth had been purchased from France and England for breeding programs in the United States.

Following the end of World War I, the Signal Corps began offering courses for its officers, as well as for other branches of the Army. By 1935, Fort Monmouth became known as "The Signal Corps School." Courses included aircraft communication equipment, telephone maintenance and operation, radio operations, radar, transmitter repair, photography, Morse Code, encoding and decoding messages (cryptography), stringing telephone and telegraph wire, and how to climb poles. Aware of the need for practical application of good communication in all branches of the Service, the Signal Corps began holding maneuvers in the late 1930s. The rapid influx of men into the military as a result of the passage of the September 1940 Selective Service Act caused many changes in Signal Corps programs and resulted in greater emphasis on training activities at Fort Monmouth. And the Japanese attack on Pearl Harbor gave every branch of the Service a sense of urgency and a resolve.

The day after Christmas 1941 I was among several hundred soldiers assembled in Hangar 1 for the purpose of choosing a training course from a selection of classes put together by Signal Corps officers: Radio Operator-Fixed Station, Radio Repairmen, Transmitter Installers, Cryptographers, and Message Center Operators.

Despite tough entry examinations, I qualified for the 13-week Radio Operator-Fixed Station course. The correspondence course I had taken with TWA in 1941, and typing classes in high school, helped throughout my progress in the course.

During the first week of school I was copying the Morse Code at 10 to 12 words per minute and enjoying the classes. About 30 students made up a class. We spent a required four hours a day copying the International Morse Code through earphones installed in cubicles especially wired for individual operators.

One morning, all trainees were marched to a big drill field for a test under simulated combat conditions. I teamed up with a cavalryman from Fort Sill, Oklahoma. He looked terrific in his shiny leggings, jodphur pants, and creased suntan shirt. As we moved across the field dragging wire, I cranked a portable hand-held generator attached to a handkey, which he used to send a message in code back to a building some 100 yards away. Then we reversed roles. Shades of World War I — dragging wire around.

Most operators could receive code much faster than they could send. Receiving over the earphones was fairly easy because of the steady rhythmic beat on prerecorded tapes. The challenge for operators was in sending at a steady pace. Sending by handkey required a firm hand, a steady beat, and proper spacing between characters. Maintaining a rhythm and properly spaced intervals between characters fatigued the arm and shoulder when sending for any length of time. Holding the key down too long on either a dot or a dash symbol screwed up the rhythm and the receiver wouldn't be able to follow the groups being transmitted necessitating a lot of repeating. Once a message was begun the rhythm had to be maintained through the complete text.

A Morse Code operator learned the distinct sound of the 26 letters of the alphabet, like listening to the chirp of different birds or notes on a piano. A five-letter group like *Amoto* was *dot-dash (**A**) dash-dash (**M**) dash-dash-dash (**O**) dash (**T**) dash-dash-dash (**O**)* (nearly all dashes). *Bishi* was *dash-dot-dot-dot (**B**) dot-dot (**I**) dot-dot-dot (**S**)* *dot-dot-dot-dot* (**H**) *dot-dot* (**I**) (nearly all *dots*). It was important to maintain the rhythm.

The old telegrapher's handkey is now a thing of the past but it once helped in the "winning of the West," and the first two world wars. Today it is a dirt road compared to the information highway.

We were taught to send messages in coded groups of five letters. A message might appear as KUHGR JPLDN NTCZO FWYMA, etc. The first two groups of five were the keys to setting up the decoding and encoding of the message. During wartime conditions, these first two groups of five were changed every morning by the War Department in Washington, D.C., and were sent to all military stations around the world.

By the time I finished the course early in April 1942, I could send at a speed of 25 wpm on a speed key called a vibroplex — an ingenious piece of equipment. I was qualified as a Radio Operator-Fixed Station. During the last days of the training, an instructor tested my skills as a receiver. He asked me to sit at a typewriter with a special groove across the top, holding a half-inch tape perforated by the code. Using a lever at my left knee, I controlled the speed of the tape as it moved across the top of the typewriter. By the second afternoon, I was reading and typing the code at 45 wpm. At the end of that day the instructor took control of the lever and I stopped typing. He instructed me to just read what was coming across the typewriter slot. During a one-minute segment, I was reading at 72 words per minute. He informed me that I qualified for a special training school offered the Army by Bell Telephone in New York City.

Alas! The next day we were mustered into six special Signal Corps detachments and put into barracks in preparation for overseas duty. Each detachment consisted of transmitter installers, repairmen, cryptographers, radio operators, and message center personnel — a total of 12 to 15 men per unit. We were capable of providing complete communication service for any combat outfit. Each soldier was trained in one specialty. I could not repair transmitters or the Hallicrafter receivers. But neither could the repairmen receive code or decode messages. The specialties complemented each other and shortened the time needed to make an effective communication team.

I was given the rank of Staff Sergeant and assigned to Detachment "T," one of six destined for the Pacific Theater of war. In the old peacetime Army it would have taken much longer to attain the level of Staff Sergeant in the Table of Organization. A new recruit remained a buck Private until showing some special aptitude or enough longevity to be advanced from a Private First Class — PFC, the backbone of the Army. A Corporal was a "dogface" who did a lot of work for Sergeants, who were constantly bucking for higher ratings. A buck Sergeant had a reputation of being an eager beaver always "bucking" for Top Sergeant status, regardless of how many rears he had to kick — or kiss. Pay for Privates was $21 per month. I sent $17 of that home to help my parents. A Staff Sergeant's pay was a whopping $55.

The sudden emphasis on specialty training introduced a whole new nomenclature into Army ratings. Detachment "T," for example, now had T4s (Technician Fourth Class), etc. I trained for a specialty that gave me a tremendous jump in pay, according to the times; however, I didn't receive the increase until I was in Australia, where I soon learned how to spend it.

One bright sunny morning our teams assembled in front of the barracks to meet our new officers — two Lieutenants to each detachment and a Captain overall. These young officers were fresh out of Officer Candidate School (OCS) and had garnered the dubious nickname of "90-Day Wonders," the length of their training course. My "Looie" was a fair-skinned redhead with fuzz on his chin. A Kansas wind would have blown him over, but he was ours to keep. Bless 'em all.

In the days that followed, we made several trips to the infirmary for shots and to the Quartermaster for clothing. Rumors that we were going to the European Theater of war were counterbalanced by rumors that we were going to the South Pacific. Because it was springtime in New Jersey, we were issued summer suntans.

One especially cold morning with no warning, we were surprised by simulated war games, an idea of the officers in charge of overseas preparedness. While the Commanding Officer and a high-ranking government official from the War Department in Washington were inspecting our detachments, sirens began screaming. Men ran into each other trying to get a look at the enemy. A flight of Piper Cubs dropped 25-pound sacks of flour on our site. Had the Japs landed at Oceanport? Or maybe Duffy's Tavern? It was supposed to give the visitor and the soldiers a feeling of combat readiness. But what a mess it was, with flour scattered everywhere. There were no trenches or bunkers to hide behind. No prior air raid instructions had been given, but we understood what they were trying to do. Some disgruntled GIs spent the afternoon cleaning up the flour as well as their pants. What an impression we must have made on the CO and the government official. It was safer back into the barracks and out of danger from flour-carrying "dive bombers."

In that "overseas" barrack I bunked with Paul Fredricks, who played second trumpet in Alvino Rey's orchestra. A few bunks away was a fellow who played clarinet in Artie Shaw's band. One Saturday morning they put on a concert in the latrine to a standing-room-only crowd of GIs. On another weekend we drove to Cape May, where they got in on an all-night "jam session." Musicians took turns improvising and ad-libbing with their instruments. On a weekend pass to New York City, we stayed in the Lexington Hotel, where I met several arrangers for some of the big bands of America. What an education I had received up to this point!

Knowing that I was destined for overseas, I filled my old suitcase with my "civvies" and souvenirs and sent it all home to Kansas. Maybe I would see them later. Then reality sank in. *We were at war and I was in it!*

Names of strange places began to appear on crapper walls and unanswered questions seeped through numb skulls. Where was Pearl Harbor? "Dumb question," a Second Lieutenant said. "It's an island off the coast of San Francisco."

Another volunteered, "It's near Samoa in the Pacific Ocean."

Thus began a lesson in geography. Pearl Harbor is a big naval base in the Hawaiian Islands and a U.S. possession. Who could forget those movies of the hula hula skirts and the "wahines."

A frequent "latrine-o-gram" concerned Australia, the Land Down Under. Down under *what*? The equator, of course. Their winter is like our summer.

Australia, I knew, was between the Pacific and Indian Oceans and nearly the size of the United States in land area. From library days I knew it raised the most sheep of any country in the world. Land of the kangaroo, the koala bear, and the platypus, Australia was famous for its Outback, big deserts, and horse racing. I couldn't understand why Australia would be in the war. I thought the war was between Japan and the United States. No one knew the answer then.

The day came when we were taken to the train station at Redbank and loaded onto a troop train for San Francisco. Some of America's finest were headed for war in the South Pacific, wondering what Australian people were like and how long it would take to get there.

Chapter 4

San Francisco, Here I Come

AT REDBANK, NEW JERSEY, on April 30, 1942, six detachments of the 997th Signal Service Company began loading into the coaches of a troop train headed west. Because no one knew our departure date, there were few relatives or sweethearts there that morning.

During the preceding days, each soldier had been issued two barracks bags, which were to become his only possessions for the duration. The "A" bag was used for carrying immediate needs, such as a shoe-shining brush and polish, changes of clothing, shoes, a mess kit, shaving kit, and personal items for everyday living. Less frequently used items, such as extra shoes, Army fatigues, a blanket, etc., went into the "B" bag. B-bags were loaded into the baggage car first, leaving the A-bags last, for quick retrieval. Living out of a barracks bag was an abrupt departure from an erstwhile normal style of living. Imagine carrying in a bag, halfway around the world for three or more years, everything you own or need for survival. No choice. One adapts rapidly.

By mid-morning, 90 restless GIs had settled into their coach seats and soon formed compatible groups in typical soldier style. Officers and auxiliary personnel were in another car. As the train moved across the Pennsylvania landscape, a feeling of excitement and camaraderie swept through the coaches. That night we slept in our GI clothes in upright seats with soldiers' legs and arms grotesquely overlapping each other. Conventional rest would have to come later.

Noon of the second day found us as guests of honor at a big banquet in downtown Chicago, a courtesy extended by patriotic city fathers of the "Windy City." I was impressed with the genuine hospitality of the occasion, and had a feeling of importance.

The third day found us chugging across the plains of Kansas, so familiar to me. Spring in Kansas is always beautiful, and the waving still-green fields of wheat made me happy but sentimental as we passed by. Our coach was filled with guys of an adventurous nature and few gripes were heard. Every day was filled with laughter and getting acquainted.

Our backgrounds were diverse and reflected America's broad immigrant base. It was fascinating to learn about each other. One tall soldier named "Buddy" had grown up in New York City's East Side. He entertained us with his survival stories. Before he was drafted, he had kept his family supplied with food by falling in front of taxicabs to collect the company's insurance money. He had sustained a broken arm, broken leg, broken collar bone, and numerous other injuries with no visible handicaps. He said it was worth it. The cabbies' insurance paid well! Another big blond Swede in our outfit had become known for his love of pickled pig's feet, which he often shared with us back in the earlier training days in our Monmouth barracks. He even brought some along on the train!

As we rolled across the broad plains of southwest Kansas in mid-afternoon, following the Santa Fe Trail, GIs sitting on the right side of the train saw a convertible full of boys racing alongside. We were approaching the town of Liberal. The youngsters sped along, like a dog chases a car, on a narrow road next to the tracks. Those young fellows waving in that pretty convertible were freedom personified, doing something boys naturally want to do when they are growing up.

The soldiers had never seen the real West before, much less so much open sky and immense open spaces. They had expected Indians and cowboys and gun fights — an image they had acquired from the movies they had seen.

When one of my detachment saw me waving to the Liberal boys with the rest of our men, he remembered I was from Kansas. He couldn't remember my first name so he said, "Old Two-gun Wyatt." From that time on, everyone called me "Two-gun."

In a little while, the train passed the city limits of Liberal and the convertible loaded with the waving boys turned into a sideroad and sat watching the rest of the train go by. The noise in the coaches never subsided as we proceeded on toward California. As our troop train left my native state, I felt badly that I had to leave my parents on a farm two miles from town on a dirt road, that wasn't too productive, and where they would have to seek help in case of injury or sickness.

At noon on the fourth day, our troop train pulled into the Los Angeles station. We fell into formation on the yard side of the station and were told we would have a five-hour layover. We were instructed to be in front of the station platform at 6:00 p.m. and sober! The Military Police knew of our arrival and would be watching us.

Los Angeles was beautiful and the weather was nice. What should we do? Two other guys and I opted to go to Robert Stack's home, one of Hollywood's stars who made their home available for servicemen. I chose Stack because he represented my kind of Western hero. During the Depression, our local merchants had put on free movies to draw the farmers and ranchers into town and maintain their goodwill, even though they were broke. Hopalong Cassidy and Gabby Hayes were everyone's favorites, though Gene Autry and Roy Rogers and Dale Evans were close seconds. But Robert Stack's movies were classy and the cowgirl interests were pretty. He was a lot more suave and cultured than Gabby Hayes.

Stack was not at home but was on location making a movie called *Badlands of Dakota* with his co-star Ann Rutherford. I remember the office in his large home was small and ordinary looking. After the conducted tour, we donned some scanty swimming togs and proceeded to fall into his pool belly-first, throwing water onto some sunbathing starlets. We didn't make a big splash with them. We were soon back cruising an area near the train station, looking for fruit stands and soda fountains to sate our appetites.

At about 5 o'clock, some members of our detachment began returning for roll call. Toward 6:00 p.m., it became comical, and a crowd gathered. Inebriated soldiers escorted by MPs were carefully stacked against the station wall, then the MPs quickly turned and went looking for more. One of the returnees was our detachment's radio repairman who was stick-stiff from too many margaritas on top of beers, which had been doctored with cigarette ashes by so-called friends. Two of his helpers carried him part of the way to the station and loaded him onto a two-wheeled baggage cart for the last 100 yards. He slid around like a hog on ice and fell off the cart several times. When the Sergeants bellowed "Fall in," he was only partially upright. Others, in much similar condition, had fallen down.

After loading on our train that night, we left the City of Angels for the City by the Bay. The next morning, we unloaded our gear at Camp Funston Training Park at Fort Mason on the south shores of San Francisco Bay. In spite of the rigorous training, I enjoyed the view of the Golden Gate, listening to the noises of the city, walking the wooden docks, smelling the many odors from small shops, and watching sailboats in the blue waters of the Bay. Did I have to leave this?

Our detachments were taken to a small school, Galileo High School, near the docks. A drill ground at the foot of Nob Hill and Van Ness Street was nearby. For the next two weeks we drilled morning and afternoon and were given lectures on weaponry . . . and venereal disease!

Between drills we were kept busy cleaning a sticky goop called cosmoline from guns, which were issued after our arrival. My rifle was of World War I vintage, a 30.03 Springfield. It carried serial number 1056235. One hasn't experienced real frustration until forced to clean cosmoline from a gun that had been buried in the stuff for years, waiting for a war to come along.

One afternoon, with the temperature in the 80s, our good Captain and the "90-Day Wonders" drilled us along the sandy beach on the south side of the Golden Gate Bridge. We were required to wear gas masks during these drills. Most revolting was marching double-time back into camp. An artillery outfit in the same school grounds wondered "who the hell" we were. And the Japs would have surrendered right then had they known about the 997th!

Except for the drilling on the beach and the drill field, I enjoyed the excitement of being a soldier now on an important mission. By the second day of our arrival, everyone had heard of the Hospitality House in the Civic Center on Market Street of downtown San Francisco. A little pamphlet entitled "Something Doing In San Francisco" explained the Hospitality House as a special place made available to all servicemen by San Francisco's mayor and city council. We had to go see it. Passes were on a rotation basis, with only half of the camp allowed out at one time. We

This booklet was given to the men temporarily stationed in San Francisco in May of 1942, before shipping out to war.

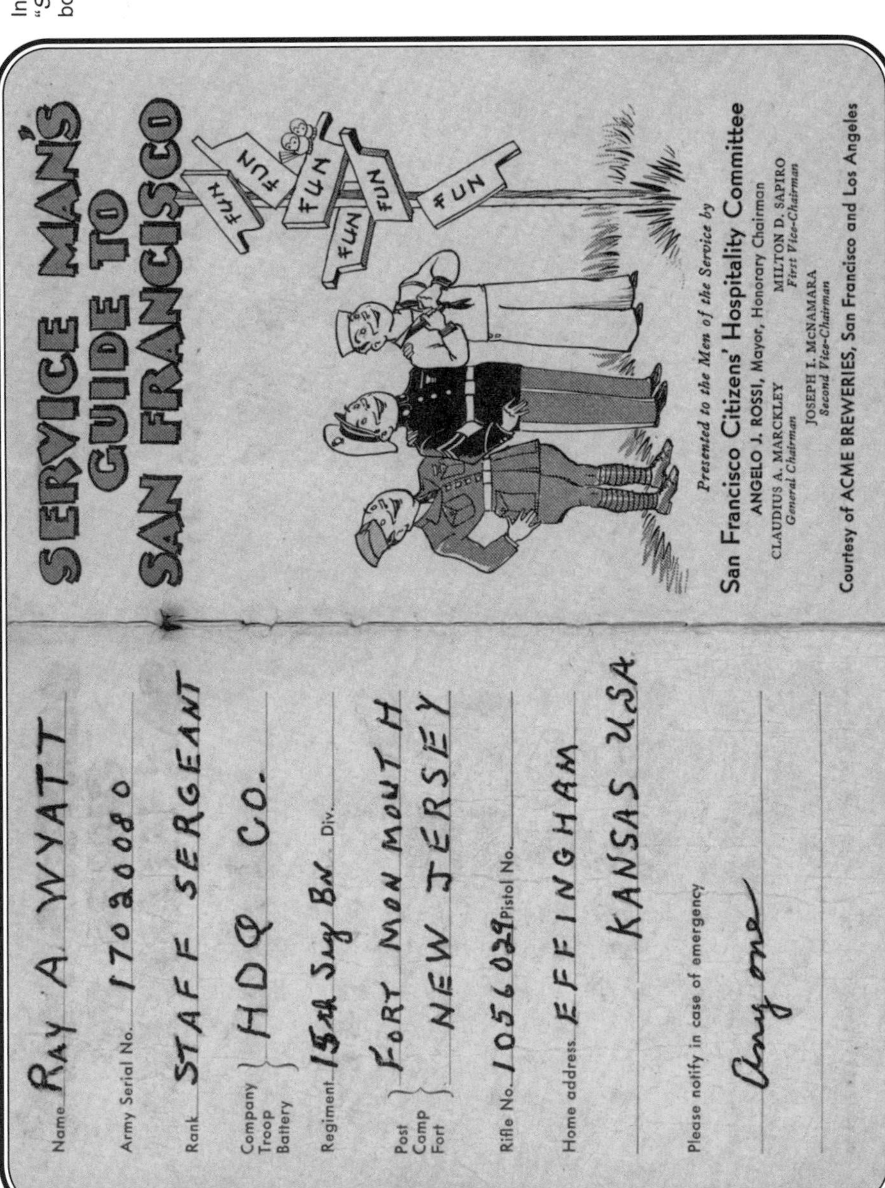

Inside cover of "*Service Man's*" booklet.

began making plans for our one good time before the word would come to board ship for overseas.

During chow, latrine-o-grams began circulating that we might be shipping out early and that passes could be canceled. We couldn't let that spoil our trip to the Hospitality House reportedly overrun with pretty girls needing dance partners. Ere the sun had set beyond the Golden Gate, we had reconnoitered the high woven-wire fence surrounding the schoolyard and planned a way out. Passes or not, we were going to storm the Hospitality House to save those damsels from boredom. A person of lesser stamina and fortitude would have taken one look at that eight-foot fence and repaired to the tent resigned to his fate for an evening of solitaire and grieving. Not so this mob of would-be commandos who wanted freedom at any price. Thoroughly scrutinizing the situation, we noticed a shed about six feet from the fence with the roof slanting level to the top of the fence. As if the Gods of Fate had taken a liking to our plans, a ten-foot plank lay beside the shed. It could be used to our advantage. Once placed across the roof of the shed to the top of the fence, we could walk the plank, so to speak.

With our escape route planned, we waited for the sun to drop into the Pacific Ocean. We were ready for perhaps our last big hurrah in beautiful San Francisco. Into our best GI togs and Army suntans, a quick dab of oil on our plumage, and a fast brush across shoe leather, we were ready to take our first beachhead. One by one the five of us nonchalantly sauntered to our rendezvous point beside the shed. Our months of drilling were about to pay off. Quickly adjusting the ladder across the shed to the top of the fence, we cat-walked the plank and dropped to the ground — free at last.

Whistling "Off we go into the wild blue yonder," the old Army Air Corps song and our all-clear signal, we ambled down the street toward a trolley stop. Climbing aboard the first available, we took seats near the door in case a sudden exit became necessary. Pleased with our progress, we were suddenly frozen by the sight of our beaming CO and a few of his "Looies." We quickly turned our backs to them. Pulling our "overseas" caps down over our faces, we gave the appearance of refugees from a zoo rather than members of the world's best-dressed army. A few elderly passengers looked at us, wondering if they were on the right trolley. As we sat like frozen statues, hunched over in our seats, my nearest buddy began choking on his cigarette. We alighted one stop ahead of our destination, to avoid the CO and his entourage.

Laughing and praising our good luck as we neared the Hospitality House, who should we see coming toward us but the good Captain. He had made one pass in front of the House, gathered a record number of salutes, and was doing an encore. Again we stirred into action. Grabbing three buxom blonds coming toward us, we proceeded to bow our heads in their midst. They were rather startled by this sudden intrusion, but began cooing with joy once they realized their unique position. They had not seen our faces, but from the back of our necks we appeared to be of masculine gender. We breathed a sigh of relief as our leader proceeded on down the street, saluting like mad. We left those girls standing in the lurch as it were.

San Francisco's Hospitality House was a serviceman's dream come true. It was manned by volunteers, including city men and women, who made extra effort to greet and guide everyone who came through the big entrances. When we heard Woody Herman's "Wood-chopper's Ball" coming from the big dance hall, we sailed right on past the table of food lined against the outer lobby wall. With girls everywhere, we spent the evening dancing to a jukebox playing all the Big Band favorites including Benny Goodman, Harry James, Artie Shaw, and "Woody."

I spent most of the night dancing with a neat brunette. At midnight, Glenn Miller's "Moonlight Serenade" put everyone in a sentimental mood. There was no hugging or kissing, just sincere goodwill and best wishes for a safe return from the war that had now enveloped the whole world.

Later, safely back at the schoolyard, we yelled, "997th Signal" to the guards as we passed through their gate. They knew who we were. I slept good that night.

The next morning another soldier and I went to Mass at St. Peter and Paul's Cathedral on Filbert Street. After Mass, the Sisters of St. Paul invited us to their dining room and fed us muffins, toast, and coffee. As we left, we walked up a few steps onto the sidewalk and made our way down the hill to the playgrounds. I had a feeling of contentment but also sensed it was our last day in the USA.

That afternoon, May 25, 1942, we packed our A- and B-bags and had our last meal before marching down to Fisherman's Wharf where the *Tasker H. Bliss*, an ocean liner converted into a troop ship, waited for us to come aboard. Now it was San Francisco, here I *go*!

Chapter 5

Goodbye USA

SAILING UNDER THE Golden Gate Bridge on the way to the war in the South Pacific with 2,400 other GIs aboard the *Tasker H. Bliss*, I wondered what was going to happen to me. Leaving the U.S. shores, bound for overseas duty, was the beginning of a greater appreciation of my country as well as a better understanding of Australia, the Land Down Under. I was leaving the security, protection, and constitutional rights of my own country. I wondered if I could expect these to be the same elsewhere. It was a benchmark in my life and an awesome feeling for one accustomed to personal freedom and justice, albeit taken for granted in America. Would I return to San Francisco and the bridge? Would I be afraid? Would I see Dad and Mom back in Kansas again?

Riding on the deck of the big ship was exhilarating, watching sea gulls and debris bobbing on the water of the Pacific, and feeling the wind and spray on my face. These were new experiences for me. Looking back at the coast of California, I watched San Francisco and the Golden Gate slowly fade in the last rays of the setting sun. Goodbye USA! We were on our way to the South Pacific to defend our country's honor and security. We were in a *go* situation. Now I really was somebody important, and not just a country boy obscured by economic conditions brought on by the drought and the hard-times of the "Dirty '30s." I was part of the "good guys" — the liberators going overseas to whip Japan into submission for their dastardly attack on Pearl Harbor. To every American, the bombing of Pearl Harbor was the same as burning the barn down on the farm or killing the neighbor's dog. That meant war.

The 997th Signal Service Company bunked below deck in the bottom hold of the *Tasker H. Bliss* next to the propellers. There was just room enough for us to walk between the beds stacked four tiers high. Nobody wanted the bottom row. Because I was the ranking soldier, I got the top bunk. Everyone tried to hang their helmet, rifle, and mess kit and toothbrush on the same bunk-posts. It wasn't safe, and we soon learned there was no sleep either.

As we sailed west into the twilight, soldiers crowded onto the top deck, partially for air and partially for sight-seeing. We were about 30 miles out from the coast of California. The sea was relatively calm, and no one was hanging over the rail feeding the fish yet. But that soon changed after our first chow, which included *ox tongue* as the main course. It looked like brisket and cabbage, but being a farm boy I knew ox tongue when I saw it. I ate it along with the rest of the meal, but some didn't, and the floor around the door of the mess hall on the lower deck of the ship soon became dangerously slick as soldiers began heading for the guard rails to upchuck. Worse, still, some of the upchuckers made it back to their bunks before chaos struck their stomachs. Some GIs spent the night on mop duty.

Rumors and latrine-o-grams detailing our destination began the first morning as the ship tacked (zig-zagged) across the ocean on a steady course toward the Southwest Pacific. On deck, strange-sounding names emerged from some of the skull sessions that usually included a member of the ship's crew perched on top of the ship's cargo. Where in the world was Guadalcanal and Port Moresby, New Guinea? Was Darwin a place or a person? Where was Rabaul and Finschhafen? I had a vague idea of Samoa and the Fiji Islands. The Japanese surely weren't interested in them. The ship continued on its steady course and the latrine-o-grams persisted.

Scuttlebutt had it that we were ship number 81 in a convoy made up of U.S. Navy troop carriers, destroyers, and cruisers now on the high seas. We were said to be the second large contingent of U.S. troops being sent

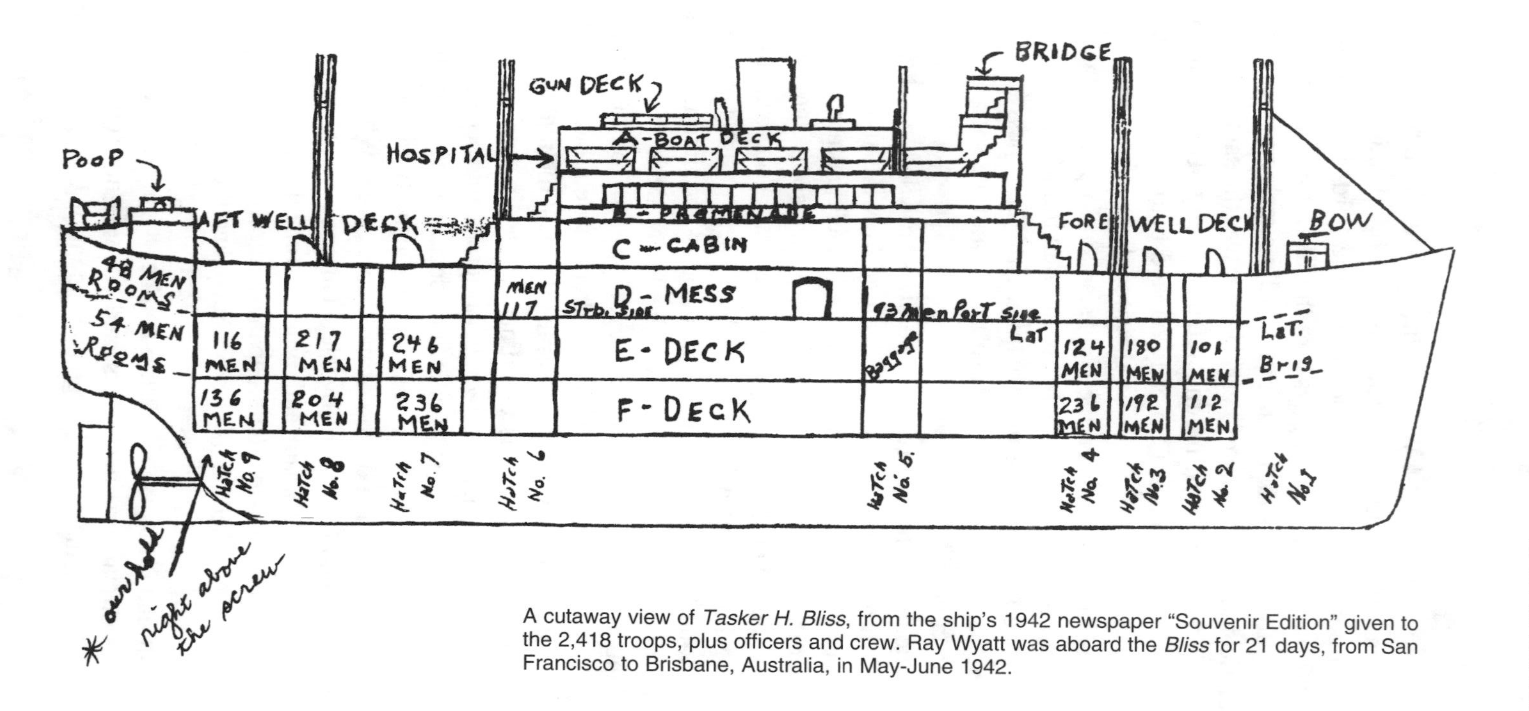

A cutaway view of *Tasker H. Bliss*, from the ship's 1942 newspaper "Souvenir Edition" given to the 2,418 troops, plus officers and crew. Ray Wyatt was aboard the *Bliss* for 21 days, from San Francisco to Brisbane, Australia, in May-June 1942.

to the Pacific Theater of war, the first having landed in Australia on December 23, 1941. I wondered where these guys got their information.

As we progressed southwesterly across blue Pacific waters, sun shadows moved across the deck at different angles as the ship tacked regularly. Now and then the sea became rough, with white caps frosting the great swells of the ocean. As I sat on deck looking at nothing but water clear to the horizon in all directions, I wondered how the natives had found and settled the many islands in the vast Pacific Ocean. I had read that they had maneuvered their outrigger canoes from island to island through this same water without the aid of a gyroscope or compass. How did they do that? I knew that navigators sailed their ships using the stars. What about daytime sailing and overcast skies in those early sailing times?

For days there were no birds, no debris, and no clouds as we sailed the blue Pacific Ocean. The heat intensified as we neared the equator. In the daytime, our quarters below deck were like bake ovens, and shady spots on the deck were hard to find. At night, the deck was a sea of sweaty bodies laying everywhere. As a "landlubber" I was glad I wasn't a sailor.

From the ship's newspaper, we learned that the Battle of Midway was being waged (June 7-8) as our convoy sailed toward Australia. All of the Dutch East Indies, including Borneo, the Celebes, Singapore, Sumatra, Borneo, Java, and Timor, had fallen to the Japanese in the two months following Pearl Harbor. Japan's conquest of the Philippines was completed, and Darwin, Northern Territory, Australia, was under constant bombing attacks. The whole South Pacific was engulfed in the war, with Japanese land and naval forces in command everywhere.

The Battle of the Coral Sea on May 7th and 8th showed that Japan's strategy was to take Port Moresby on the south coast of New Guinea and thus cut the supply lines of the United States to Australia. Messages intercepted earlier at Bataan revealed that the Japanese intended to take the harbor of Rabaul (New Britain), Port Moresby (New Guinea), and Tulagi, an island off of Guadalcanal — all part of Australia's Mandated Territory of New Guinea. But the Battle of the Coral Sea saved Australia and preserved the supply lines that allowed the productive might of the United States to be poured into all parts of the Pacific war. Though neither side claimed a victory, that naval battle was a turning point in the defense of Australia and the beginning of a turn-around in the South Pacific conflict. Japan's defeat at Midway gave *us* command of the sea. And the Japanese navy was never a big threat.

Halfway around the world, Hitler was winning his bid to conquer all of Europe, and the United States was faced with supplying troops and war matériel to two fronts, both of major importance and immediate concern. It was indeed a world war. I was apprehensive as to what the consequences might be if we did not win.

As we sailed along on the good ship *Bliss*, our days were filled with drills, gymnastics, and chow lines. On weekends there were church services. Other days we listened to lectures and pep talks by specific officers and read the ship's newspaper. Free time on deck allowed us to get in a snooze or watch the card and dice games. Occasionally flying fish, breaking through the top of big waves, came sailing in among the troops on board ship. At night, electric eels followed alongside the ship like hungry puppies. And every evening it was "LIGHTS OUT" and "NO SMOKING ABOVE DECK."

One Sunday morning before church services, a priest was hearing Confessions. That seemed like the right thing to do, so I got in a line where a priest was leaning over the guard rail as he listened to his petitioners. There were five or six guys ahead of me, and then I noticed they weren't interested in confessing. They had weak stomachs and were upchucking over the edge. I soon got into the right line . . . the one leading to God.

One soldier attracted a lot of attention. He was of medium build and had a pock-marked face and a noticeable separation in his front teeth. He and his pal, a smaller dark-haired guy, had grown up in Hollywood. They were in an outfit called the "airborne infantry." According to them, they were to be flown into enemy airfields and do as much damage as possible to planes and ammunition dumps. No plane would return to pick them up. That impressed me. What was so fascinating was that he was the filthiest talking man I had ever encountered in my sheltered life. He recanted the crudest sexual acts imaginable with Hollywood stars and extras. He described in detail the acts of sex deviates and the misuse of the reproductive process. He said he and his pal had survived in that manner. This farm boy listened with fascination, disgust, and disbelief to the lurid descriptions he and his cohort related to all who could crowd around them. I saw him again later in Australia, but under different circumstances.

Most of the guys aboard ship were regular run-of-the-mill types who loved their mothers, bragged about their hometown, and were always ready for a game of sandlot ball. They were mostly patriotic Americans constantly looking for places to sleep, insistent on fair play, and not likely to be pushed around. I liked these eager, clean-cut guys. I felt they could each perform their job, and together we made a team.

Gambling was the most popular activity on board ship. Every day, in every shady spot of the top deck, groups gathered on spread-out Army blankets. They were shooting craps mostly. Sometimes other groups gathered around the edges making side bets. I had never seen so much money in my life. I soon caught on and bet a guy that the dice roller would make his point. I lost.

One fascinating fellow looked like a typical riverboat gambler. He had coal-black hair, clean olive-textured skin, and long slim fingers. He parted his oily hair down the middle and slicked it straight back. His smile was artificial and useful when he wanted to make a point. Once when he saw me eyeing him, he flashed a friendly smile. He probably had never seen a plowboy like me before. He was older than most of us by 10 years, and he warned us green kids not to get into a game of cards with him. Most everyone was in the Service to get a job done and to go back home and pursue a career. Not this guy. He already had a career . . . gambling. He didn't think overly much of fighting some warlord, and he made no bones about it.

He didn't talk much. Bullets could have been flying all around him and he would still be concentrating on what he was doing and who had an ace in the hole. I couldn't believe that everyone was not interested in fighting the enemy and in defending our country. Yet he probably would make it back home without a scratch — and tell other farm boys not to gamble unless they knew the game.

As we neared port, the size of the little group of gamblers became smaller and the game was between fewer and fewer participants. All of the money was in the hands of two or three guys. On the last roll of the dice, the money piled on the blanket for the winner totaled some $5,000.

After 23 days tacking across the Pacific to avoid Japanese submarines, the *Tasker H. Bliss* put in at Auckland, New Zealand. I was up early that morning. Through the blue-gray mist I saw debris floating on the water and the silhouette of land off the port bow. Land Ho! Soon Auckland, New Zealand, was fully visible.

Even life aboard ship didn't stop Army routines. At first light, each day's duty assignments were posted. On the day we arrived at Auckland I found that I was the Sergeant-in-Charge of latrine duty on our end of the ship, the aft, and just above the screws (propellers) of the ship. As I peered out the porthole on the starboard side, the ship began slowing down in the calm water inside the harbor. Suddenly, overhead, a two-motored bomber swept in low over our bow. I learned later it was an Australian Beaufighter. It dropped bombs and zoomed up into the sky ahead of us. Some GIs just above me on deck began cheering. They reported that the Beaufighter had hit a Japanese submarine there in the harbor. Sure enough, as we moved forward, I saw an oil slick beginning to bubble up as we passed over the spot. It was a close call. Scuttlebutt again had it that three submarines had been sunk after our convoy left San Francisco. We were in a war!

After we had docked in Auckland, a crowd of civilians and New Zealand soldiers gathered alongside our ship. They began tossing fruit up to us and asking for money. We obliged by inserting coins into the fruit and throwing it back to them. It was a happy occasion and nothing like I had envisioned or had been led to expect of these island people. The countryside back of the harbor was beautiful, and a church tower was visible in the distance.

Then a strange thing happened. New Zealand police and some of our ship's personnel escorted about two dozen men in civilian clothes aboard. I had never seen mutineers! They had refused to man their ship for fear of its being sunk in Pacific waters. They were to be turned over to naval authorities in Brisbane, Australia, our destination.

The *Bliss* pulled out of Auckland an hour before sundown and was making a dash across the ocean under cover of darkness in order to avoid Japanese submarines, according to crewmen. It was miserable down in the hold that night. In their haste to get across to Brisbane, the *Bliss*'s command pushed the ship beyond normal operational speed. Grease around the screws stiffened, due to the excessive heat, and reduced the vessel's speed. The ship vibrated all night, making sleep difficult. The heat and lack of ventilation nearly suffocated us. Some men upchucked, but were not allowed above deck.

The dawn saved us. When we emerged on deck the next morning, we were greeted by the skyline of Brisbane. We had reached Australia, our ally, and our destination.

Chapter 6

Welcome to Australia

BEFORE WE COULD go ashore at Brisbane, our ship was put under quarantine, an international maritime rule. Harbor medical officials came aboard and verified that there were no infectious diseases among us. We had made it to Australia under wartime circumstances.

Our first footsteps on the Land Down Under were planted at Ascot Racecourse inside Brisbane's sprawling city limits, but we weren't there to see the races. Ninety men and their A-bags occupied racehorse stalls lined with fresh straw bedding — for the horse, of course.

Arrangements for chow had been made ahead of time by a group of GIs dispatched previous to our arrival. The first question from America's conquering heroes was, "What are the women like?"

Next question, "Can I get some leave time?"

One of the cooks replied, "This is a great country and the girls speak English. Be sure and stop at the Pig and Whistle." He didn't take time to explain.

It took a day to make camp and get our A- and B-bags sorted. Following chow, a couple of us applied for passes. Late in the afternoon we caught a tram from Ascot to downtown Brisbane. A big river flowed through the very center of the city of approximately 500,000.

We took in a roller-skating rink, where after a few busted butts on the surface of the rink we were able to cruise upright. As darkness fell, we made our way back to the racecourse, stopping at the "Pig and Whistle Cafe" for a new discovery — a crumpet. It was a round, doughy biscuit warmed over and sopped with butter. We washed it down with a cup of tea. I was used to thinking only in terms of coffee, hamburger, and milk shakes. The Australian "sheilas" who waited on us were openly astounded by this new horde of America's finest. Indeed, we had landed in Australia and the natives were friendly!

The "Land Down Under" the equator was an English-speaking country full of friendly people. For Yankee soldiers meeting the "fair dinkum Ahs-strile-yun" was an adventure to be remembered. Australians were our cousins from the old country — the mother back East from whom we emigrated to different countries and for different reasons.

Real Aussies were a free thinking, fun-loving mob of daredevils who exhibited uncommon bravery and dedication to duty and yet were a bunch of blokes who took time to "boil the billy" — enjoy a cup of tea — no matter what extraneous circumstances prevailed.

In 1942 we became allies for a common goal: the survival of our countries. American servicemen needed only to hear the encouraging words, "Gud on ya Yank" and we got "stuck into it" together to push the enemy back to his homeland some three years later.

I could never figure out how they came up with the word cobber, meaning a friend. A cobber was a friend, but a mate was a . . . well, a mate — and not necessarily a real close cobber. Americans were "fair dinkum cobbers" when the going got tough. But sometimes a mate wasn't really a cobber, but someone who might be in the way or impeding progress, as in "buzz orf, mate," or "Gud on, mite." Too right!

On our second day in Australia, early that morning, we loaded onto a passenger train bound for our ultimate overseas destination — U.S. Headquarters Base Section Four in Melbourne, Victoria. Another Staff Sergeant and I were in charge of the baggage detail. Everyone was in good spirits as our train left Brisbane headed south. Early in the afternoon as the troop train rolled along, we passed through pretty wooded country and over a body of water called the Hawkesbury River south of Sydney. Looking out of the windows, we saw oyster beds planted in some of the coves. The operation was explained by one of our own countrymen.

Before sundown we reached the Queensland-New South Wales border where all the baggage had to be unloaded and reloaded onto another railway with a different gauged rail (the distances between iron rails) — a quirk in Australia's rail system. As darkness obscured the Australian countryside, our slow-moving train continued south toward the state of Victoria.

Four soldiers shared one cubicle of our coach. We spent most of the night thrashing and turning in that boar's nest filled with cigarette smoke and foul odors. We were unprepared for our next introduction to Australia. Standing stiff-legged in the door of our cubicle was an Australian soldier. We wondered how he had finagled a ride onto our troop train. He was wearing a gorgeous big hat with a turned-up brim onto which was pinned a black emblem of bristling bayonets. Calling himself a "fair dinkum Aussie," he was eager to inform his captive audience of his country's ways and mores. Because I admired his unique military hat, he forthwith offered it for sale. Had I bought it then, it would have had an uncertain future in my jungle experiences in New Guinea.

I wasn't prepared for the strange language that poured forth from our obliging new friend. A mop of curly red hair poked out from under his big hat. He said his name was "Bluey." We learned this was a typical exaggeration of Australian speech. A blond was nicknamed "Whitey" and a curly haired bloke was naturally "Curly." My oath!

"Fair dinkum" or "dinkie di" meant something was on the level and a fact. A "sheila" was a girl, and a "bloke" a male Aussie. We told "Bluey" he talked kind of funny. He fired right back. "Jest talkin' Ahstrine, Mite. Blimey! Your ears must be a bit crook." Seeing we weren't following him too well, we offered him a pack of American cigarettes. He nearly tore his pocket off trying to get to his money, but we refused to take it. He said, "Ta," meaning thanks, a dozen times while inhaling big drafts. Then we asked him how the war was going with the Japanese. To show his bravado, he let loose a string of oaths, but the only one I understood was, "Too rite. Too bloody rite, Mite."

When I told Bluey I had been a cowboy, he seemed pleased, and then quickly explained that in Australia cowboys are called "jackaroos" and a cowgirl is a "jillaroo." A "mob" was a big bunch as in a "mob of sheep or cattle or 'roos" (kangaroos). Bluey told us that a kookaburra was a bird much like our American kingfisher. Because of its piercing, raucous call, it was called a laughing jackass in Australia. Thus the name . . . kookaburra.

Money is the first thing to be reckoned with by a soldier in a new country. He is dead in the water without purchasing power. By popular demand, Bluey became our authority on Australian's financial exchange. We asked him about the paper money and hard cash issued to us when we first encamped in Ascot racecourse in Brisbane.

Bluey explained that the smallest in value was the copper "'awpenny" or half-penny. This was followed by the big copper penny. Then came the three-pence called a "thrupence," then the six-pence called a "zac," and then a shilling, a silver piece about the size of our quarter. Two shillings made a florin. Their paper money was called a pound or quid and was written like a forward slanted L. On a piece of paper he showed us how the price would appear on something we might buy, especially a pot of beer. It would look like this: £/s/d, which stood for pounds/shillings/dinars (pence). All we really needed to know was that six shillings and one pence (6/1d) equaled one American dollar. The pound note (£) equaled 20 shillings and/or $3.75 in the 1942 rate of exchange. Later we learned that we would be paid in 5-pound notes (100 shillings) and 10-pound notes (200 shillings). Silver coins were important to remember. Just forget about filling your pocket with the copper stuff. The largest size coin was the copper penny, designed to be easily grasped in one's pocket or purse. According to Bluey, it was the most frequently used coin in the old days because so many purchases cost only a penny.

Our military pay would always arrive on time, and we would try to ignore the "haypenny" and go for more "pounds."

Our talkative "cobber" — our friend — was oblivious to where he was or what time it was in our little cubicle as our train made its way across the Australian countryside. He had kept us awake into the morning hours.

Shortly after dawn, we pulled onto a siding in Aubury, a little town on the northern border of Victoria, where we off-loaded from our smelly cubicles and into U.S. Army 6x6 trucks (six wheels on each side) headed for Melbourne. Then Bluey disappeared from our lives wearing his beautiful hat, with a trail of smoke from an American cigarette floating out behind him.

Our new camp was in a grove of eucalyptus (called gum) trees in beautiful Royal Park on the edge of Melbourne. New clean tents had been set for us by the Australians. We slept on new Army cots, with four men to a tent. It was terribly cold at night. Even Chicago's railyards the past December or the blizzard aboard the Santa Fe "Red Ball Freight" had not been as frigid as those tents in Melbourne.

There was an explanation. We had left San Francisco in summertime and were wearing suntans and lightweight clothing when we boarded our ship back there. June and July in the Land Down Under was wintertime. Though it didn't snow in Melbourne, the chilling night air and the humidity made it miserable. I slept with all my clothes on while wrapped in an Army overcoat and two blankets. I was still cold and spent the night praying for the dawn. A week later we were issued our winter clothing.

In the morning for our breakfast we experienced the Australian "mess." With no previous warning, Australian army cooks fed us mutton stew, the odor of which permeated the whole building. We were rescued from a steady mutton diet by a member of our detachment who had gotten a pass and located a so-called Comfort Station. There, for a couple of shillings, one could get a meal and a hot shower. Australian army exchange stores, as we knew army exchange stores, stocked very little that would tempt a hungry Yank.

Our Detachment, "T," of the 997th Signal Service Company, bivouacked in a eucalyptus grove between downtown Melbourne and Port Phillips, 22nd Port of Embarkation. It rained every day that June and July. We traversed from tent to mess hall, then to the latrine, on floating wooden sidewalks especially made for the Australian wet season. American chow was available to satisfy our appetites, but the damp cold nights prevailed.

Company assignments were made and the reason we were in Australia began to dominate our thinking. Japanese troops were in the islands north of Australia, and the Japanese bombers continued unabated their raids on Darwin in the Northern Territory. The enemy seemed unstoppable, and an unspoken fear gnawed at the conscience of Allied soldiers as well as citizens on the streets of every Australian city and village. City officials in Melbourne ordered trenches dug in beautiful St. Kilda Park, a disheartening blow to the pride of the people in Melbourne. Would the Japanese actually invade Australia?

Australia needed General Douglas MacArthur and his great stone face. Early in March, when President Franklin D. Roosevelt had ordered the

An American troop convoy in a eucalyptus grove on maneuvers in Australia, 1942. *Commonwealth of Australia, Department of Information*

General to leave the Philippines and go to Australia, a reluctant MacArthur, his family, and some staff members were taken to Mindanao in the southern Philippines. From there they were flown to Batchelor Field south of Darwin, Northern Territory, Australia, and eventually made their way to Melbourne.

From the Hotel Australia, General MacArthur began the task of pulling together the Allied forces, including the first contingents of the U.S. Armed Forces in Australia that had already arrived soon after Pearl Harbor. Australia's best fighting men were supporting Churchill's embattled armies at El Alamein and Tobruk in the Libyan desert in North Africa and on the Island of Crete. Others, Australia's 8th Division, with 16,500 men, had been captured in Singapore and were in Japanese POW camps. And small elements of the Australian army, navy, and air force were scattered throughout islands of the Mandated Territory of New Guinea. All of Australia's available military strength alone could not have warded off a concerted enemy attack on their homeland.

Before General MacArthur arrived in Australia, ABDACOM (American, British, Dutch, and Australian Command) had been destroyed in the Battle of the Java Sea, and the Japanese controlled the Indian Ocean as well as most of the sea lanes of the South China Seas. In Washington and London, the decision had been made to concentrate on defeating the German armies first while MacArthur was to somehow stabilize and hold the advance of the Japanese to the islands north of Australia.

The General's reputation and professional record were the catalysts that united the Australian people behind their leaders and their Allies. MacArthur's leadership generated the resolve Australians sorely needed to stop what they believed to be the inevitable invasion of their homeland. General MacArthur's image, exemplified by his stern jaw, corn-cob pipe, and deliberate stride, was his greatest contribution to the Southwest Pacific war in its early stages.

Often criticized, General MacArthur made decisions and assigned military commanders on the basis of availability and proven leadership and experience. Before he took command, the Australian Chiefs of Staff were committed to defending Australia on Australian soil. Because of great distances, inadequate communications, and lack of a continental railway, General MacArthur's strategy was to prevent the Japanese from ever setting foot in Australia and to fight the enemy at the perimeters of the island continent. His Allied Command concentrated on the defense of New

An early contingent of U.S. soldiers drill somewhere in Australia.
Commonwealth of Australia, Department of Information

Trenches were dug in St. Kilda Park in downtown Melbourne as a precautionary measure. This photo was taken from the ANZAC (Australian-New Zealand Army Corps) Memorial, August 1942. *Ray Wyatt photo*

Guinea, especially Port Morseby, and Guadalcanal, in the Solomon Islands, adjacent to the Bismarck Archipelago.

Had the General not made it out of Corregidor on March 11, 1942, during the Japanese takeover of the Philippine Islands, the campaign to drive the enemy back to Japan could have failed later. The Japanese's propaganda advantage would have killed the spirit of the defenders of freedom and slowed the effort to drive the enemy back to their homeland.

Despite his uncertainty over his next move, and chaffing from President Roosevelt's order that he leave the Philippines, MacArthur took command of an unorganized situation in Australia that demanded immediate remedies and strong action.

Australians idolized the man and looked to him as their savior in a world suddenly in danger of extinction. What course might the war have taken had this image of leadership and strength of character not been forthcoming at this historic moment? It could have been a long war and even disastrous to freedom-loving nations around the world.

At the end of the war, some time later, on August 6, 1945, Howard Pyle, a good friend and future governor of Arizona, was one of seven war correspondents at General MacArthur's Manila headquarters the afternoon of the Hiroshima atomic bomb drop. Pyle subsequently wrote the Tempe *Daily News*, February 27, 1981: "During a personal briefing by MacArthur the man left little doubt that he was opposed to the use of the bomb."

The air war over Japan had seen 800 B-29s blast the enemy with 6,000 tons of blockbusters and fire bombs. A complete blockade surrounded Japanese home islands that had been almost impregnable.

The Japanese had been ordered to surrender unconditionally. On August 10th they requested less severe terms, including the proviso that Emperor Hirohito retain his power. The Allied response was that the Emperor must take orders from the victorious powers. After three days, on August 13, 1945, the Japanese government accepted the peace terms.

At the conclusion of General MacArthur's briefing to correspondents there in Manilla in 1945, Pyle asked, "What chance do we have for a lasting peace when all of this is over?"

General MacArthur's reply: "There will be no enduring peace among the peoples of the world until our destructive genius is outrun by worldwide success in developing character in man."

The General was right.

Have we developed character in the men of this century?

When the Japanese failed to take Port Moresby and Milne Bay by sea, which had been their main objective in the Battle of the Coral Sea on May 7-8, 1942, they opted to land troops at Morobe, Lae, and Salamaua, along the north coast of Papua New Guinea. Then in July 1942, Japanese troops began an all-out effort to take Port Moresby by way of the Kokoda Trail over the Owen Stanley Mountains from Morobe. It was a bad decision on their part. The unexpected disastrous effects of dysentery, jungle rot, malaria, leeches, heat, and exhaustion in an impenetrable jungle affected both sides. The fierce fighting and determination of Australian and American soldiers on the Kokoda Trail made a big difference in the outcome of the New Guinea campaign. Lack of sea lanes, starvation, exhaustion, and scant medical supplies forced the Japanese to abandon their New Guinea campaign in December 1943. Allied victories at Midway, Guadalcanal, and Hollandia, coupled with immense build-up of Allied supplies lines, gave us the advantage.

Long supply lines directed at too many fronts brought about the beginning of the end of Japan's conquest of the Pacific. After the loss of Guadalcanal in the Solomons Islands in February 1943 and the Battle of the Bismarck Sea north of Finschhafen on March 3rd, the Japanese did not attempt to land troops anywhere in New Guinea, but began to withdraw back toward the Philippines.

During the summer of 1942, Australia's eastern coastline became the staging area for the Southwest Pacific Theater of war. In Melbourne, the Commanding Officer of the 997th Signal Company made assignments and the war took on a more somber meaning for American overseas troops. I was assigned to Base Section Four Signal Center in Melbourne as a radio operator.

Finally, I was able to contribute to the war effort.

Chapter 7

Melbourne, Australia

MY FIRST assignment as a radio operator at Melbourne Base Section Four that summer of 1942 was in a small room that housed a Hallicrafter receiver, a transmitter control panel, and a message desk. Nearly all of the Base Signal Center's communications was by teletype and phone then. The radio code station was for standby only, in case of emergencies, and for communications with stations with no telephones. I was responsible for the total operation of the radio section.

With no previous training in station management, I started calling phone numbers left on my desk. Luckily, I got the transmitter station near Ballarat where our antennas were located. I learned from the transmitter personnel that I was to call our transmitter station each day as the sun went down and ask them to change frequencies for nighttime broadcasting. Every evening, as the ionosphere changed, radio waves striking ion layers in the solar system at differing angles caused the signals to fade and good reception was impossible. The transmittermen had to be notified each evening to go to a different frequency. I used one frequency to receive messages and a different

Ray Wyatt (l) and Frank Novotny on their first night off, on Swanston Street, Melbourne, Australia, June 1942.

Trams on Swanston Street, Melbourne, were the main mode of transportation when U.S. servicemen arrived in 1942. *Ray Wyatt photo*

The author, Raymond A. Wyatt, at his equipment, with the 997th Signal Service Company in the South Pacific.

one for sending. Thus, I tuned in the other stations on their new frequencies, and they looked for me on my new frequency. This operation kept me busy, but since the radio section was for standby only and not vital, my input was minimal and temporary. On my time off, I explored the city of Melbourne.

I loved Melbourne, with its long line of trams (trolley cars) on Swanston Street and the ambiance of a busy metropolis. I liked to walk up Collins Street past USAFIA Headquarters to the Australian Comfort Station, like our USOs in America. Big Clydesdale horses clopping along the cobblestone streets pulled wagons loaded with wooden kegs of beer. It brought to mind the movies I had seen of New York in the early 1890s. I tried to imagine our beer being delivered in America by horse-drawn wagons.

Melbourne imposed a 6 o'clock curfew on beer in its pubs and grog shops each evening. A dignified city, Melbourne was proud of her British theaters, her financial base, her sophistication, and her affluence. Citizens on the street stressed that they were not part of the original convict element that had settled Sydney in 1788. Those British rejects had been sent to Australian shores by the mother country. Brisbane, Queensland, was populated by the same class of original settlers as those in Sydney. Melbourne citizens did, however, concede the fact that Sydney had the most beautiful harbor in the world and gorgeous beaches to match her blue Pacific setting. Sydney possessed an ambiance and hustle-bustle reminiscent of San Francisco in the Gold Rush days.

Melbourne and Sydney had an on-going argument over which was the larger city and which rendered the most state and national leadership. Both claimed to have over 1 million population. Total population of Australia in 1940 was near 7 million. In comparison, the population of New York City at that time was over 14 million. Nearly 75 percent of Australia's citizens lived east of the Great Dividing Range that stretched along the coast from Townsville to Melbourne.

Any day in Melbourne one could encounter small Afghan camel drivers, Maori soldiers from New Zealand, "diggers" selling uncut opal stones, and vendors who were Chinese, Italian, or Greek. Occasionally, a half-caste aborigine mingled into the usual mix of Australians in one city block. Melbourne's international flavor was the result of its financial climate and good seaport at Port Phillip. There were no panhandlers evident on Melbourne's wide streets.

Australians made full use of their free time with recreational pursuits such as horse racing, surfing, and keeping the pubs and grog shops profitable. The Melbourne Cup Day, known in racing circles around the world, was a national holiday. I visited the Museum of Victoria in downtown Melbourne, where a replica of Australian racehorse Phar Lap was on display. Phar Lap once had raced in California, but was believed to have been poisoned because of his threat to American racehorses. Whether this is a proven fact or just fiction of an international competition turned sour, I don't know. In addition to horse races, Australians developed their own brand of football called Australian Rules Football, or "Footy," right there in Melbourne.

A favorite meeting place for Yanks and Australian girls was under the big clock at Flinders Street Railway Station by the Prince Bridge over the Yarra River. There were no traffic lights in that city of 1 million people, and cars drove on what we thought was the wrong side of the street. Each time our American vehicle passed through a certain busy intersection, the jolly Australian cop would begin his little prance while whistling "Yankee Doodle" as he waved us on through.

Yanks Down Under during the war in the South Pacific listened to the finest music. Radio stations and programs were owned by the Australian and British governments. There were no commercials, just nice quiet music with no interruptions.

In contrast, nearly all American commercials in the States were presented with some musical jingle and always too loud — a U.S. trademark. Australians who listened to American programs thought we were daft and a bit brassy with our commercials, but they liked our GI jive.

It was in Melbourne that I first saw the bobbies — beautifully uniformed policemen riding bicycles and carrying billy clubs. On special days and during parades they rode well-groomed horses to break up crowds. I found it hard to believe that these bobbies could stop criminals from robbing banks and pulling holdups on the wide streets of such a large city. One morning, as I waited for another serviceman at a prearranged corner of a bank in downtown Melbourne (I think it was on Bourke Street), I saw many people, young and old, going into and out of the bank, carrying small leather cases that looked like they might contain the receipts or operating capital for the day's business. I thought what a time America's Dillinger or Capone would have in Australia, and wondered if the bobbies would even have a chance of apprehending such characters.

It would have been easy to snatch any one of those small suitcases and disappear into the crowd on the busy street. I asked a bobbie friend about the susceptibility of robbery and other street crimes in his city. Did he feel safe? Could he stop a criminal?

"My word," he said. "We just don't think about it. We're not inclined to crime like you Yanks. We don't need to carry destructive weapons on the street here. You Yanks do because you think that way."

But I still wondered why it was that criminals had not over-run the thrifty, placid city of Melbourne. Of course, there wasn't that much petrol available for robbers, even if they had a getaway car.

Melbourne taxis were fueled by charcoal burners attached to the trunks of the vehicles like big bunsen burners with live coals. Some cabs carried large bags of gas strapped to tops of vehicles like loaves of bread.

The city's night life shut down early, and the last tram from downtown was at 10 o'clock. Allied soldiers often missed the tram and had to walk the three or four miles back to camp each night. Meat pies and "lolly" water — soft drinks — were the only snacks available to Americans accustomed to a menu of hamburgers, malts, bacon and eggs, and hot coffee.

One of the numerous Comfort Stations was "The Dugout," on Swanston Street. It was a favorite meeting place for all Allied servicemen because of the hospitality and the live band. The Dugout closed each night with "Now is the Hour," the beautiful farewell song of the Maori of New Zealand. It was at The Dugout that I heard "Waltzing Matilda," Australia's national song, for the first time; I soon learned the words and their meaning.

> Once a jolly swagman camped beside a billabong
> Under the shade of a coolibah tree,
> And he sang as he watched and waited 'till his billy boiled,
> You'll come a waltzing Matilda with me?
>
> (Original lyrics by A. B. (Banjo) Paterson)

The translation goes something like this: A jolly swagman is like America's happy hobo. A swag is his bedroll, which he called Matilda. Strapped over his back, it contained all his personal possessions. A billabong is a small pond. A coolibah is a kind of Australian tree. A billy is a tin can used to boil water into which is dropped tea leaves for a siesta, called a "coffee break" in the U.S. "You'll come a waltzing Matilda with me" is an invitation to his swag to come along as he swings out across the bush, or Outback.

The song is more than a catchy tune. The lyrics describe the classic conflict between property owners and the laboring class in every society around the world, the *haves* versus the *have nots*. In the song, the swagman killed a drover's jumbuck (sheep) near a billabong for something to eat. He is arrested and rather than give up his carefree life, dives into the billabong and drowns. Like America, the Land Down Under suffered years of depression and economic hard times and many took to the highways and the Outback respectively to survive. Thus the song illustrates the sentimentality of both the producers in society and the laborers or downtrodden. The song favors the downtrodden — the swagman and his "Matilda." Like the United States, Australia in the '30s and '40s had a lot of swagmen.

We had been introduced to the language of Australia by our cobber, Bluey, in the first days following our arrival. He had also explained their money, but it didn't mean that much to me because three-fourths of the time that I was overseas I was not near a cafe, a drygoods store, or a movie. Since there was no place to spend money, I sent most of my paychecks home to help Mom and Dad.

Within one month after my assignment to Base Four, the radio station was discontinued and I was assigned to an intercept station — copying the enemy's messages — attached to General MacArthur's Headquarters. Working intercept was a fascinating and new experience for which I had not received training at Fort Monmouth's Signal Corps school.

Among the men who escaped from Bataan with MacArthur in 1942 was a Master Sergeant Messer who had worked intercept in the Philippines before the Japanese struck Manila. Sergeant Messer's job was to set up the same kind of operation at Base Section Four in Melbourne for the General's G-2 (Government Intelligence). Working intercept called for skillful operators and experienced cryptanalysts. Radio operators and cryptanalysts operated in separate rooms at all times.

From l to r: Sergeant Clarence Young; Master Sergeant Messer, chief of intercept operations at General Douglas MacArthur's Headquarters; and Staff Sergeant Wyatt, August 1942, at Melbourne. *Ray Wyatt photo*

Radio operators never knew the content of the coded enemy messages they took down. The first two groups of five characters were called key groups, the ones daily sent by the War Department in Washington to all military communication centers around the world. The operators' copies of the coded messages were given to cryptanalysts who decoded and sent the English version on to the Central Bureau of Intelligence, Chiefs of Staff, and command posts around the world. The Central Bureau of Intelligence added the collections of information from the many operators and branches of the Service before sending it to the chiefs and generals who made the decisions that would affect the outcome of the war.

In our own messages, places and campaigns were given code names in order to confuse the enemy. Keeping everyone informed as to where to hit the enemy and with how much was a complicated matter and an intriguing part of conducting a war. Most of it began with radio operators on board ships, or in the many outposts in the theaters where the war was being fought.

Describing the victory at Midway, Admiral Chester W. Nimitz attributed much of that success to "the men who toiled underground at Station Hypo at Pearl Harbor," who broke the enemy JN-25 naval code before the Japanese attacked the island.

On September 2nd, I was assigned to Sergeant Messer's new intercept group. We began the operation in a room with no windows, like our high school band room back home, on the second floor of a school in the heart of Melbourne. There were three walls full of Hallicrafter receivers operated by 20 to 24 radio operators. We began monitoring every code station around the world. We scanned every frequency, from medium frequency band waves (300 to 3000 kilocycles) to very high frequencies (30 to 300 megacycles), and recorded each station's call letters, frequency, and signal strength. After a week of monitoring, we began copying only those stations beginning with the letter J — for Japan. I copied JAP-JAN Tokyo, and JAP-JAB Batavia, now called Jakarta, in Java. These stations were not too difficult to copy because of their low mellow tone, which I had gotten used to. Their transmissions were coming over at a slow 25 to 28 words per minute. The code for JAP-JAN's call letters was *dot-dash-dash-dash (***J***) dot-dash (***A***) dot-dash-dash-dot (***P***) hyphen dot-dash-dash-dash (***J***) dot-dash (***A***) dash-dot (***N***).*

Then one morning, without warning, the code signals changed. There were some signals with as many as four and five dots and dashes. I had never heard a *dot-dash-dot-dot-dash* or a *dot-dash-dot-dot-dot* in Morse Code. Master Sergeant Messer noticed I was having difficulty, and he was getting uneasy because I wasn't copying as I normally did. He stood behind me and listened. The code seemed to have additional dots and dashes trailing each letter of our Morse Code. I thought it was a garbled transmission, and checked my frequency on the Hallicrafter receiver. I was on JAP-JAN Tokyo. But I was unable to type what I was hearing.

I told the Master Sergeant, "I'm confused. I can't get it. I don't know what it is."

"Stay with it," he said. "Copy it just like you're hearing it. It's Japanese *Katakana* code. They're combining two letters of our alphabet."

After about one week of practicing, I was able to recognize some of the two-letter groups — which actually were one character in *Katakana*. I

ン n	ワ wa	ラ ra	ヤ ya	マ ma	ハ ha	ナ na	タ ta	サ sa	カ ka	ア a
	イ i	リ ri	イ i	ミ mi	ヒ hi	ニ ni	チ chi	シ shi	キ ki	イ i
	ウ u	ル ru	ユ yu	ム mu	フ fu	ヌ nu	ツ tsu	ス su	ク ku	ウ u
	エ e	レ re	エ e	メ me	ヘ he	ネ ne	テ te	セ se	ケ ke	エ e
	オ o	ロ ro	ヨ yo	モ mo	ホ ho	ノ no	ト to	ソ so	コ ko	オ o

Example, using the letter A

Morse code: ._ .__ ._ ._. ._ _.__ ._ __ ._

A W A R A Y A M A

(note the break between letters)

Katakana: .__._ ._.._ _.__._ __._

Wa Ra Ya Ma

(no break between letters) Try chanting the *Katakana* — a different sound (phonetically *dash dot* is *dah dit*).

Thomas Kadomoto

Katakana was a set of symbols for syllable writing of Japanese *Kana*, dating from the 8th and 9th centuries. *Kana* is either of two different but equivalent sets of characters that are used in the *Kana* system; each have 48 characters, increased by the use of two diacritics to 73.

Only 22 to 25 were used in the messages Ray Wyatt had intercepted. The English vocabulary has 26 letters, with a corresponding Morse Code symbol (*dit dah*) for each letter. An operator learns these codes by a particular sound for each letter — like listening to notes on a piano. Example: A station calls another by sending CQ (*dah dit dah dit dah dah dit dah*). If you try saying that faster and faster, it become a rhythm and a sound.

When the Japanese began sending their *Katakana* code, Wyatt knew that it was not the English alphabet. The Japanese were adding vowels onto a set number of consonants.

easily recognized certain letters of our Morse Code, such as the K, N, T, S, H, etc. The Japanese added vowels — A, E, I, O, U — to a consonant to make a new sound or character.

International Morse Code used 26 letters of the English alphabet. *Katakana* code reportedly had 73 characters, accomplished by combining two of the letters of the alphabet into many combinations. I recognized the letter K, *dash-dot-dash*, then heard *dot-dot*, an added I. Combined they made Ki. A *dot-dash-dot-dot-dash*, turned out to be Ra on my typewriter. Besides the regular 26 letters in our alphabet, I learned an additional 22-25 letters of the *Katakana*. Others that I picked up on were Ka, Ke, Ku, Ki, Ko, Ta, To, Se, Su, So, Na, No, Ho, etc. Our Remington and Royal typewriters did not have these combined letters, but the Japanese-

	ガ GA	プ PU
イ I	ヨ YO	コ KO
ロ RO	タ JA	ゴ GO
ハ HA	レ RE	エ E
バ BA	ソ SO	テ TE
パ PA	ゾ ZO	デ DE
ニ NI	ツ TSU	ア A
ホ HO	ヅ DZU	サ SA
ボ BO	ネ NE	ザ ZA
ポ PO	ナ NA	キ KI
ヘ HE	ラ RA	ギ GI
ベ BE	ム MU	ユ YU
ペ PE	ウ U	メ ME
ト TO	ヴ V	ミ MI
ド DO	ヰ WI	シ SHI
チ CHI	ノ NO	ジ JI
ヂ JI	オ O	ヱ YE
リ RI	ク KU	ヒ HI
ヌ NU	グ GU	ビ BI
ル RU	ヤ YA	ピ PI
ヲ WO	マ MA	モ MO
ワ WA	ケ KE	セ SE
カ KA	ゲ GE	ゼ ZE
	フ FU	ス SU
	ブ BU	ズ ZU
		ン N

END OF MESSAGE QUOTE

The Japanese *Katakana* radio code. *Department of the Navy*

American cryptanalysts downstairs had equipment with five rows of keys to accommodate these characters.

The most frequently used letters in the English language are E T A I O N. In Japanese, some of the most often used are O T I M W and A. The least used are Q X Z. In the *Katakana*, the O I A M U and K seemed to be used the most. The Japanese were sending in groups of five, just as in our Morse Code groups. But because of the added vowels, I sometimes ended up with eight or nine letters to a group.

Our Japanese-American cryptanalysts knew how to handle those groups. These Japanese-American soldiers had been trained in Hawaii before the war, and after Pearl Harbor were kept under Military Police guard, which we thought unfair. We gave them a friendly wave in the hallway each evening as we passed their room. They decoded the *Katakana* and hand-carried the information to MacArthur's Headquarters, so that the General was getting his G-2 some two to three days before it was reported to other units and the news media.

Breaking the code (cryptography) is accomplished by analyzing the frequency in which certain letters appear in the language or code used in the radio operator's copy of the transmission. After a period of time we could recognize the sameness and frequency of symbols and letters of the alphabet and construct a sentence.

Eventually special machines, the *Enigma* in Europe and the *Purple Machine* in Japan, made it possible for warring nations to change codes and develop new ones in a never-ending battle to keep the advantage and the enemy off balance. These encoding machines incorporated the use of rotors so that a sending key on one became a different key on the receiving machine. World War II was a time when many code aficionados tried to invent an unbreakable code.

Our interceptions there in Melbourne ended up in our Intelligence Bureau in Washington and in other Allied Headquarters where our High Command conducted the war against the enemy. The Japanese as well as the Allies changed their code regularly, and the air was full of strange combinations of signals, some meant to be true, others decoys.

Our contribution in Melbourne was minimal, however, compared to the U.S. Navy's skilled operators and cryptanalysts who were so important in the outcome of the war in the Pacific. We only copied the coded messages; we never knew what they contained. Yet, I felt that in Melbourne we contributed to Intelligence centers around the world, and I had a part in the success of the war in a special way, thanks to Master Sergeant Messer.

While I was still on intercept, I experienced the phenomenon called triangulation, a trigonometric operation for finding a location by means of bearings from two fixed points a known distance apart. One morning during a coffee break a group of us were near a receiver that began a noticeable vibration. The Master Sergeant ran to the receiver and fine-tuned it so that the signal was coming in loud and clear. The letters MARU were repeated several times. These letters appeared on the sides of Japanese ships and were used for identification. The Master Sergeant asked that one of us swing our directional antennae around until he got the strongest signal, from a east-northeast direction. He then called the Royal Australia Navy and gave them our location in miles, the strength of our signal, and the direction of our strongest signal. Using the same technique, the RAN picked up the same letters and reported they had a fix on the object.

Picture a triangle. Using the distance between our two stations as the base of the triangle, find the two strongest signal positions on each of our directional antennae as the sides of the triangle; the point where these two signals crossed would be the location of the object. The RAN was able to determine the point where the two sides of the triangle crossed or came together. The source of the signal turned out to be a Japanese ship just off the coast of Australia and east of Melbourne. Our triangulation had been useful and effective.

We went back to copying code, and we never learned what action the RAN took against the Japanese ship. For diversion, I copied other stations, and one morning intercepted a declaration of war between Brazil and Germany on August 22, 1942.

I worked intercept for four months, during which time MacArthur's Headquarters moved north to Queens Street in Brisbane as the war intensified in the Solomons and on the northern coast of New Guinea. In late December, USAFIA Headquarters decided to send a mobile radio unit to Darwin at what was called the "Top End," in the event the Japanese invaded Australia's Northern Territory. I and two other Signal Corps men got the assignment. We were about to experience Australia's famous Outback — like no other place on earth.

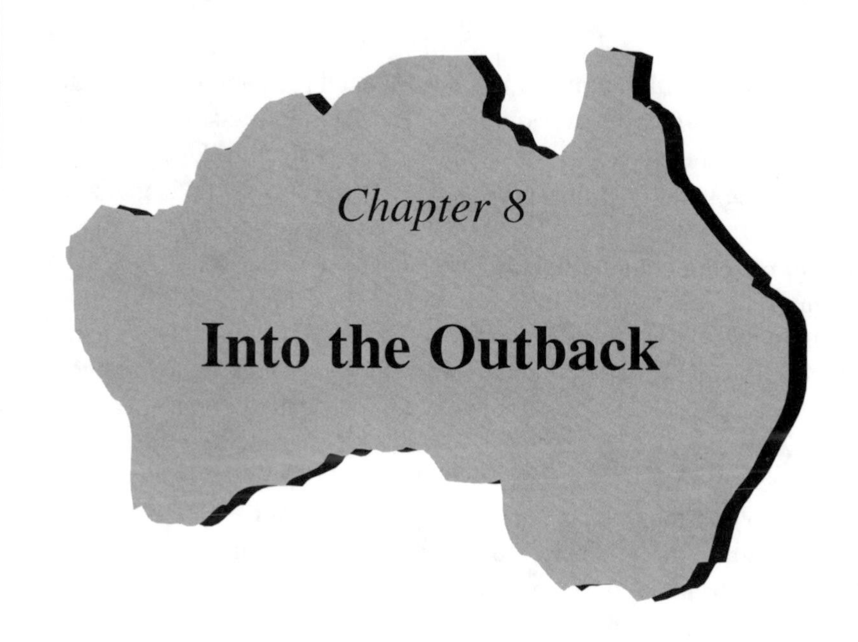

Chapter 8

Into the Outback

A CENTURY AGO, Australia's Outback was all of the country west of the Great Dividing Range along the east coast, encompassing nearly three-fourths of the continent. Words cannot adequately describe the heat, the dryness, the isolation, and the nothingness of what Australians simply called the "Outback." In this vast area of red dirt, scrub and bush, drought-ridden deserts, and inadequate water supply, the only inhabitants were isolated groups of aborigines, half-castes, and some of the most rugged individuals on earth, the "diggers" — men looking for different kinds of minerals scattered on the ground or in rough outcroppings. The Outback contained some of the world's largest cattle ranches, as well as gold, silver, copper, lead, bauxite, opal, and iron mines, all of which entailed the biggest gamble on earth.

Less than a dozen small towns had a population of over 1,000 in a vast area as large as the entire Western United States in 1942.

In late December 1942, the two Signal Corpsmen and I left for Darwin, on Australia's northern coast, to deliver the mobile radio unit — a complete radio station built on an Army 6x6 truck. General MacArthur was taking no chances. He wanted communications maintained in the event the Japanese overran Darwin and northern Australia. Our route would take us across Australia in much the same manner as going from Florida to Seattle by way of New York. But our military training had not prepared us for the Outback. No officer, no civilian, no map maker or scout could have explained what lay before us.

In 1860, Australian explorers Robert O'Hara Burke and William John Wills attempted to find a north-south route from Melbourne to Normanton, through north-central Australia, by way of Birdsville. They failed in the end because of poor communications. Like those early explorers, we had no highway maps, no tourist pamphlets, no city chambers of commerce literature to prepare us for what appeared to be a routine assignment.

The day after Christmas 1942, we loaded our duffel bags onto the freight train carrying our mobile unit, left Melbourne station, and headed up Australia's eastern coastline. December was summertime in Australia. The weather was nice and living was easy. There were no bullets to dodge, and our billfolds were full of Australian money.

About 100 miles north of Melbourne, we stopped at the little town of Albury at the Victoria-New South Wales border. After checking into a rustic two-storied hotel, we swam in the town's spacious pool across from our hotel. As we crossed the wide street in front of the building, we were forced to stop for a drover leading his horse across — memories of Effingham's main street in Kansas. While we slept, our mobile unit was off-loaded from the Victoria line and reloaded onto the New South Wales line, which had a different rail gauge.

That first morning we found that our mobile radio unit was loaded near the engine of the train. Climbing aboard, we took a position on the outside of the unit for security. For most of the morning we chugged along up the eastern side of the Great Dividing Range going toward Sydney. The landscape had a golden cast, similar to California's sun-burnt hills, caused by dead grasses from a summer's drought. The soft-sloping hills and tall eucalyptus trees across the Australian countryside were knee-deep in grass in all directions. We moved across the vacillating countryside with nary a sign of human activity. No houses. No towns. No automobiles. And no hamburger joints. There was no livestock grazing the area. Just miles and miles of rolling hills and gum trees. Our train was the only sign of life.

A crew of jolly "diggers" ran the small steam engine, No. 5244, fired

The Hotel Australia in Albury, Victoria. Sergeants Young, Johnston, and Wyatt stayed here while their mobile radio unit was off-loaded from Victoria rails onto New South Wales rails in December 1942. *Ray Wyatt photo*

Ray Wyatt on the way to the Outback, riding Engine No. 5244, on January 1, 1943. He was in obvious good health at the time, weighing 170 pounds. *Ray Wyatt photo*

Ray Wyatt standing beside small Australian freight cars on the way to Townsville and Mount Isa. The photo was taken on New Years Day, 1943, in the Brisbane railyard. *Ray Wyatt photo*

These bullocks were used to pull the train up steep hills or to help start momentum up grades. Note the log chain connected to the freight cars from the bullocks.

Ray Wyatt photo

by logs of gum trees. No coal or petrol was available in wartime. The train consisted of about 20 flatcars, including our mobile unit. On the morning of the first day, at about 10 o'clock, the train slowed to a snail's pace then came to a halt. I wondered what had caused it to stop in the middle of nowhere. Was there a kangaroo on the tracks? When I ran to the engineer at the front of the train he handed me a cup, "'Ave a cup of tea, Mite!"

This was my introduction to the practice of the "billy," a sacred ritual in the lives of "fair dinkum" Aussies that I had heard sung about in "Waltzing Matilda." Blimey! A war was going on and lives were being lost. But there in the Outback we were "'aving a cup of tea!" My oath!

No. 5244's "billy" was a gallon tin can filled with water, heated on the side of the steam engine's boiler. Tea leaves were dropped into the boiling water. Thus was I introduced to a unique and relaxing custom . . . the boiling of the "billy" and the break that goes with it.

During my first "billy" break, the engineer and his fireman, a young, wide-shouldered bloke with fair skin, told me about the railways in their country. He assured me that their railroads were much safer than those in the United States. On their system they carried the only key to the switch to the next town on the track. Since there was only one track, no other train could possibly be on the same track as they. We went chugging across the Outback, safely, as if time and the world were on hold!

Toward noon of that second day, we skirted around the west side of Sydney, capital of New South Wales and largest city in Australia, though Melbourne disputed that claim. After a brief pause in Sydney we went on to Brisbane, capital of Queensland, where we laid over a day and a night while the yardmen once again switched our cars and equipment onto another gauge. We had come across part of Victoria, crossed New South Wales, and now Queensland on our third different gauged railroad. We were experiencing a military logistical nightmare. The Victoria rails were 5 feet, 3 inches apart, the New South Wales rails were 4 feet, 8½ inches apart, and Queensland's rails were a narrow 3 feet, 6 inches apart, necessitating off-loading and reloading at each state border. It was not a fast way to move freight or troops a long distance!

We spent New Year's Eve 1942 in Brisbane's railyards. On the first day of 1943, we were again traveling up the eastern coast of Australia. That evening I experienced the real Australian Outback in a scene that even Hollywood movie makers could not have planned or staged.

At sundown, as our train slowed to a crawl, we entered a big grove of gum trees under which a big mob of horned cattle was being mustered. Some drovers and jackeroos leisurely rode between the train and the cattle, whose hooves churned up a thick cloud of rose-tinted dust that hung heavy over the tops of trees. Above the animals' disgruntled bawl, I heard a kookaburra's raucous cry. There it was in one scene. All of the lore that made the Australian Outback what it is was happening before me: the drovers, the jackaroos, the mob of bellowing cattle, the kookaburra, and the gum trees. All was visible in that dusty-red shrouded sunset. Missing were a kangaroo, a dingo, a jolly swagman, and a billabong.

As our train moved slowly out from the lowland, we passed a large group of small tents pitched on a hillside beside the tracks. The train crew told us the tents were inhabited the year around by railroad workers who maintained the tracks. Once again my mind wandered back, to memories of Boy Scout camps in the open countryside back home.

The following morning we were several hundred miles north of Brisbane and close to the ocean. I remember the train stopping at the edge of Machay, a pretty little town whose main street reached clear to the water's edge. It would be an appealing place to live after the war.

On the third day, we met some Australian soldiers who had loaded onto the train back at Brisbane. Their outfit was called the "25 pounders," the weight of the shell fired from their two-wheeled cannons. I think they were from the Australian 9th Division that had just returned from fighting Rommel, "the Desert Fox," near the port of Tobruk, in Libya, and El Alamein, in Egypt. They were the heroes in Britain's defense during the North African campaign.

As part of Britain's commonwealth, Australia and New Zealand troops were thrust into action in the battles in Europe nearly two years before the Japanese attack on Darwin and Singapore. Now back in Australia, and without much rest or recuperation time, these troops were being rushed into action at Milne Bay, Port Moresby, and Morobe off the northeast coast Australia. They were the sons of the real Australian "diggers."

We next spent an hour's layover in Townsville, where I saw my first Japanese prisoners of war, handcuffed and bare from the waist up. The sight of them brought me closer to the reality of war. Also in the station was a tiny lady dressed in a kimono. I guessed her to be Javanese or Timorese.

Townsville had the dubious distinction of having been bombed by the Japanese in what was a scare tactic designed to show Australians that their country was vulnerable. It only intensified Australia's war effort. Townsville and Cloncurry, in upper Queensland, became staging areas for the U.S. military personnel sent to support Allied troops in New Guinea and the Solomon Island campaigns.

Leaving Townsville, we went past Charters Towers, a U.S. airbase, and headed west for Cloncurry, where Australia's first flying doctor service had been started in 1917. Dr. John Flynn, then a Presbyterian missionary near Alice Springs, saw the airplane as a way to service the medical needs of people in outlying areas of Central Australia. His foresight and dedication in alleviating the suffering of many who would have perished in a harsh land earned him a place in the hearts of Australians.

After passing Cloncurry, our train came to Mount Isa. I couldn't believe the isolation. Desolate Mount Isa reminded me of some Colorado mining towns. The tailings of a big mine said to be owned and operated by an American ran around the south side of the tiny town of 500 or 600 people. The mine was producing silver, lead, and zinc. I remember Mount Isa because it was the end of the railroad. Only one rough dirt road led off west into the bush from that point. Mount Isa was the end of civilization

Australian trucks of the Aussies' "25 pounders" (cannons) loaded on rail cars headed for Townsville. Australian "diggers," who manned these trucks and guns, had just returned from the North African Campaign and were now being put into the New Guinea Campaign, January 2, 1943. *Ray Wyatt photo*

and everything related to human existence. From there on, the Outback was *far* out.

The Captain of our Signal Corps detachment met us at Mount Isa and directed the unloading of our mobile unit from the train. We found an Australian supply dump and filled the truck's tank with petrol for the impending journey to Birdum, on the U.S. Base Section One Headquarters. But Birdum was still 1,000 miles away up a narrow, bulldozed, desolate, and rough dirt road.

We loaded onto the floor of the mobile unit a box of Army K-rations and material for making our own coffee. We carried two five-gallon cans of water on the back of the truck — our only supply of water for our trip. There was no shade anywhere, no Comfort Stations, and few humans for those next 1,000 miles. It was into the wild bush yonder, cloudless skies, and an endless dusty road through the scraggly Northern Territory. We were in "never-never" land from there on.

January was the hot time in this tropic zone, and thus we wore Army suntan cutoff pants and no shirts. There was no saluting and no need to

Some of Australia's "25 pounders" on the way to New Guinea. Wyatt was proud to stand beside them on the railroad north of Brisbane, January 2, 1943.
Ray Wyatt photo

At Mount Isa, the truck and mobile radio unit were readied for the 1,000 miles across the Outback. Ray Wyatt is on the right.
Ray Wyatt photo

This page and opposite: Australian workers camp north of Brisbane in the real Outback, January 2, 1943. *Ray Wyatt photo*

Above: The only road across the top half of Australia in January 1943 was from Mount Isa, Queensland, through the Northern Territory to Darwin, at the "Top End." A truck on the horizon coming toward the men is barely visible. The author followed 1,000 miles of this corrugated, dusty road, in a 6x6 Army truck loaded with a mobile radio shack and a portable generator on a trailer.
Ray Wyatt photo

Left: Yanks drove on the wrong side of the road in Australia — even in the Outback. *Ray Wyatt photo*

A road through the Outback near Darwin during the monsoon season. Note there are no telephone poles or road graders' marks. *Ray Wyatt photo*

U.S. Army Headquarters Base Section One at Birdum, Northern Territory, flying "Old Glory," in January 1943. *Ray Wyatt photo*

The tent area of Base Section One, Northern Territory, at Birdum was known for flies, heat, and inadequate living conditions. There was no "Company Street."

Ray Wyatt photo

The radio tent at Birdum. The equipment consisted of (l to r) a 100-watt transmitter, a typewriter, a speaker on top of a Hallicrafter receiver, and a vibroflex speed key (shiny metal object on the desk) for sending code. The pin-up girl on the receiver is Myrna Loy, the Hollywood star. The stuffed kitten on top of the speaker was a Christmas present from home. The large square speaker on the extreme right was a public address system. *Ray Wyatt photo*

The medical tent at Birdum. *Ray Wyatt photo*

The mobile radio shack served as the quarters for the men throughout the long trip across the Outback. Radar, the terrier, stayed with Ray Wyatt clear to Darwin.

Ray Wyatt photo

The "Joey" baby kangaroo, and Radar, our dog. Note Radar's splinted left front leg.

Ray Wyatt photo

follow Army regulations. We were on our own and not on a set schedule. Our job was to get that mobile radio unit to the Northern Territory and into civilization again as soon as possible.

At daybreak on a hot January morning, the Captain, two Tech-Sergeants, and I crowded in behind the wheel of the groaning Army 6x6 truck and headed toward Birdum, on the north-south track to Darwin.

We were on a bulldozed graveled road about 15 feet wide that earlier had been graded by U.S. Army engineers. Like a heat-rippled mirage, the road ran in a straight line for as far as one could see, with not one tree or shrub to break the monotony of the landscape. It is hard to describe 1,000 miles of no activity — nothing. Placed at strategic locations along the road were petrol stations equipped with wreckers and emergency equipment. The men at these outposts were in the first stage of going "Tropo," a state of mind in which they climbed trees, but there were no trees. We saw nothing but dust, blazing skies, and a hot, rough road for two days. We took turns driving and sleeping on the floor of the mobile unit and the seat of the truck.

Maps of Australia's roads showed only one crooked line running from Mount Isa to the north-south track to Darwin. We estimated we were about a third of the way to our destination. We drove only during daylight hours because of the uncertainty of the roadbed and the would-be drain on the truck's battery if we used lights. It had been more than a week since we had left Melbourne.

About noon of the third day out, we noticed a strange cloud of dust off on the far horizon. It was an odd sensation after seeing nothing but a straight line of lonely road for days. Was it a mirage? The cloud came closer, until it boiled up over our truck. There in an American jeep, in the blazing sun, sat an Australian soldier grinning from ear to ear. He was bareheaded, red-faced, and three-sheets-to-the-wind drunk. He was wearing cutoff tan pants, unbuttoned shirt, and knee-high socks. Beside him in the passenger seat were six quart bottles of brown liquid, which I quickly recognized as Plonk. The Australians called it Plonk because after a couple of swigs of that stuff one went "plonk" on the floor! My brother used to make it from the dregs of beer and fermented grapes; it was to be avoided if possible.

Our red-faced ally was very friendly and insisted we have a drink with him. We deferred to our Captain who was a man with a ministerial background. He declined, and seemed to lose his composure for a moment. He sensed the abnormality of the situation and felt he should report to someone regarding a lost jeep and an inebriated "digger"! But where in that God-forsaken country would one report anything?

When we declined the invitation, our ally promptly roared around us, heading east toward Mount Isa. The mystery of where he had come from, if the jeep was in fact stolen or if he was AWOL, remained unsolved. But that Australian left a memory of what freedom was all about. To hell with the war! His freedom was what he was fighting for.

After some 500 miles across the Outback, small scrub and dwarfed trees began to appear. Short-leafed grasses also began to fill the landscape under small trees and desert washes. During the whole trip I had not seen one bird or animal — not even a kangaroo, dingo, or rabbit. The first critters I spotted were wild, unbranded cattle, called "clean skins" by the drovers.

Staring continually at nothing for days would test anyone's stamina. The stark realization that we were in the middle of nowhere, devoid of even the simple amenities of a natural existence and no evidence of civilization, began to gnaw on us. There were no buildings to break the skyline and no noise save the roar of our truck and our own voices. Such mind-boggling desolation produced a robotic reaction in us, and sleep was something we could only dream about.

Late in the afternoon of the fourth day we came to a squatty, corrugated-roofed building off the road about 100 yards among some gnarly trees. The grass was beaten down for some distance around and the soil was hard-packed around the single door. One of the T-Sergeants and I left the truck to investigate, hoping to find fresh food and some lolly water to drink. Stepping inside the dimly lit room, we noticed a long bar running clear across one wall and the rest of the room void of furniture. It was a typical Outback pub. The customers were road construction workers, a few Australian soldiers, some jackaroos, and a drover or two. The Sergeant and I carried our own mess cups, a trick we learned during the 6 o'clock beer curfew in Melbourne.

As we leaned against a wall grasping our "pot" of beer, we observed the noisy crowd of Australians enjoying their favorite pastime. Suddenly a loud shout erupted over the din of laughter and noisy conversation followed by the rapid drumming of a tin cup from the end of the bar nearest the door. Standing belly-up to the bar was a slightly inebriated, overweight, red-faced soldier shouting, "'Ow 'bout it, Mite? Do I bloody well get a beer or do you cop this bloody bomb?" In his right hand, in a characteristic stiff-armed maneuver, he grasped a familiar checkered object — a hand grenade! The two soldiers nearest him hit the floor. The rest along the bar began descending in a ripple effect until the whole room was in a squatting position and silence prevailed.

He got his beer quickly. Gulping it down, he backed out the door. "She'll be right!" he said as he disappeared into the bush.

The war was brought much nearer. I learned years later that this was a place called Three Corners, where the Barkly Highway meets the north-south track to Darwin. We were on the Stuart Highway, the north-south track through the center of the continent. It was the only road for approximately 2,200 miles of mud or dust, and bogs and potholes, between Darwin on the north and Adelaide, South Australia. These rut-filled roads were not for the faint-hearted bloke or even a stout-hearted Yank.

Finally, we pulled our mobile unit into Birdum. We left the mobile unit and the generator at a Headquarter's tent where the American flag was flying in the Australian breezes. There, scattered among the bush and kunai grass, were a dozen tents for the men and their equipment. The Signal Center had the nicest tent in that overgrown bush campsite. Two signalmen were there to man just one radio operator's position. Radio traffic was light, and it seemed the war had moved on toward Australia's Top End.

The first morning after our arrival in Birdum I reported for sick call. By my recollection, the trip from Melbourne had taken two weeks. During that time, with no water for showering, I had a week's accumulation of red dust mixed with sweat over my entire body. Dermatitis had erupted on my genitals, and a rash made me itch all over. I was one worried Signal Corps soldier when I walked into the Medico's tent that morning.

A young fellow stepped out from behind a large box filled with cubby-holes of bottles and dressing material resembling a chuck wagon cook's kitchen back home on the range. When I stripped down, I was almost in tears. I was sure he had never seen anything as swollen as me. I was really worried. I couldn't go home like this.

The doctor looked at my pain-wracked face and grinned, "You'll be all right. You'll have to go to the field hospital for a few days."

I spent the next week on my backside, soaking myself with a disinfectant and hot water — no big deal, but scary.

Chow time in that God-forsaken, fly-infested, humid, hot, overgrown jungle was a real treat. The cook baked something with chocolate every day, insisting that it was a good source of energy. What a guy! I wondered how he ended up in this lonely outpost. We could look forward to chocolate cookies, chocolate brownies, chocolate cake, chocolate rolls, and other equally tasty treats. He was a cheerful fellow, about 30 years old and a former chef at The Palmer House in Chicago. I hated to leave there. I hope he got home okay.

While at chow one day I saw my first aborigine. He was a burly, energetic fellow wearing a large floppy hat and an unbuttoned short-sleeved shirt. He was threshing through the bush on the trail of some nondescript cattle we called "okies" — or Oklahoma mavericks — back in the Kansas stockyards. The Northern Territory seemed to be overrun with unbranded cattle.

After hazing — driving — the cattle out of sight, he returned to our mess hall to see who we were and to check the breadbox. He had deep-seated black eyes under heavy protruding eyebrows. His high cheekbones highlighted a wide bulbous nose over a mouthful of perfect white teeth. He was wearing big stockman boots and dirty dungarees. With him was a typical, slim Australian jackeroo.

A swarm of tiny flies, the likes of which I had never seen before, followed them through the bush. Flies covered the nets hanging from their hats and around their necks, and the two men seemed to accept them as part of the occupation. Their horses were also covered with flies.

After filling their stomachs there in the mess hall they took off in pursuit of the mavericks. I would encounter more of these "black pellas" later, but that day I returned to my hospital bed, amazed at what I had seen and the good food I had eaten in a setting right out of a book.

There was no company street in our Birdum bush camp. Tents were scattered around under the eucalyptus trees. It was all shrubs and small trees, and every man for himself, though each tent was connected by little paths through the tall grass.

One morning after breakfast in the mess hall, I returned by way of the Casual Tent, a tent for GIs in transit to other posts. There were ten cots in the tent and an aisle down the middle. Mosquito netting hung suspended from supports over each bed, and it was hard to see if the cots were occupied. The sun shone only about half way across the floor, putting many of the cots in the shadows. As I stepped through the doorway carrying a mess kit in my right hand, I saw a blue and grey python fully 10 feet long stretched out across the floor. The snake's head was up and pointed toward a foot protruding from under the mosquito netting of a cot. I yelled, "Snake!" as loud as I could and hurled my mess kit. I missed the snake, but the noise distracted it. It slithered into the grass at the end of the tent.

When the guy in the cot heard me yell, he stuck his head out and then quickly pulled his leg back inside the netting. His face turned a ghastly white as he watched the snake disappear into the bush. That soldier was out of his cot in a flash and began blabbering to the crowd that gathered that he had been attacked by a python 25 feet long. The size of the snake grew with each telling. I would have liked to read his letters to friends back home.

When I left for overseas, I figured the tropics would be full of snakes, lizards, and wild animals. It did not turn out that way. Evidently the vibrations from heavy equipment and thunder from gunfire, bombs, and heavy weaponry caused most of them to recede into the bush and jungles to avoid extermination.

After my stint in the field hospital there at Birdum I was ready to move up the track to Base Section One Headquarters, now at Adelaide River. There we bivouacked in 6- to 8-foot kunai grass. Whole tents could be hidden in the grass, and there was no company street. A guy could have gone "bush" and spent the war hunting kangaroos. (There may be some guys still in that tall grass!)

January was the monsoon season there, and it was wet and humid all of the time. At the Headquarters warehouse, 100-pound sacks of sugar turned into hard sugar cement. We were fortunate in that we kept our little rounded logs of leftover Christmas candy to sweeten our coffee.

For a belated Christmas present, U.S. Armed Forces officers promised turkey dinners to all GIs in the South Pacific Theater of war as an appreciative gesture to the enlisted men so far from home on that traditional day. With great expectations, sparked by so many rumors of the impending banquet, we cleaned our mess kits and waited for the mess hall summons. Alas and alack! What was billed as turkey turned out to be Australian

The American Army camp in the Northern Territory on the only north-south track from Darwin to Alice Springs and Adelaide, South Australia, 1942.
Ray Wyatt photo

Two Yanks boiling their clothing at a petrol supply dump in the Northern Territory, Australia. *Ray Wyatt photo*

hare! I know a jackrabbit's hind-leg when I see one, and especially when I taste one. For a few tough years during the "Dirty '30s" in Kansas our family had survived on rabbits and cracked wheat. But the Army's intent was there, and some soldiers who didn't know any different enjoyed the "turkey" and lolly water as though it were a feast from home. The dressing and the cranberries were good. It was the official gesture that counted.

Adelaide River was a busy place and even boasted of a cinema — a bunch of logs lined up in front of an outdoor screen. Once or twice a week we could see Roy Rogers and Dale Evans or Fred MacMurray, if the theater wasn't closed due to wet weather. The monsoon season was hot and suffocating both day and night. Three radio operators kept watch 24 hours and handled lots of messages.

The U.S. Army Signal Corps Center at Adelaide River (above) and Birdum (below), Northern Territory, January 1943. *Ray Wyatt photo*

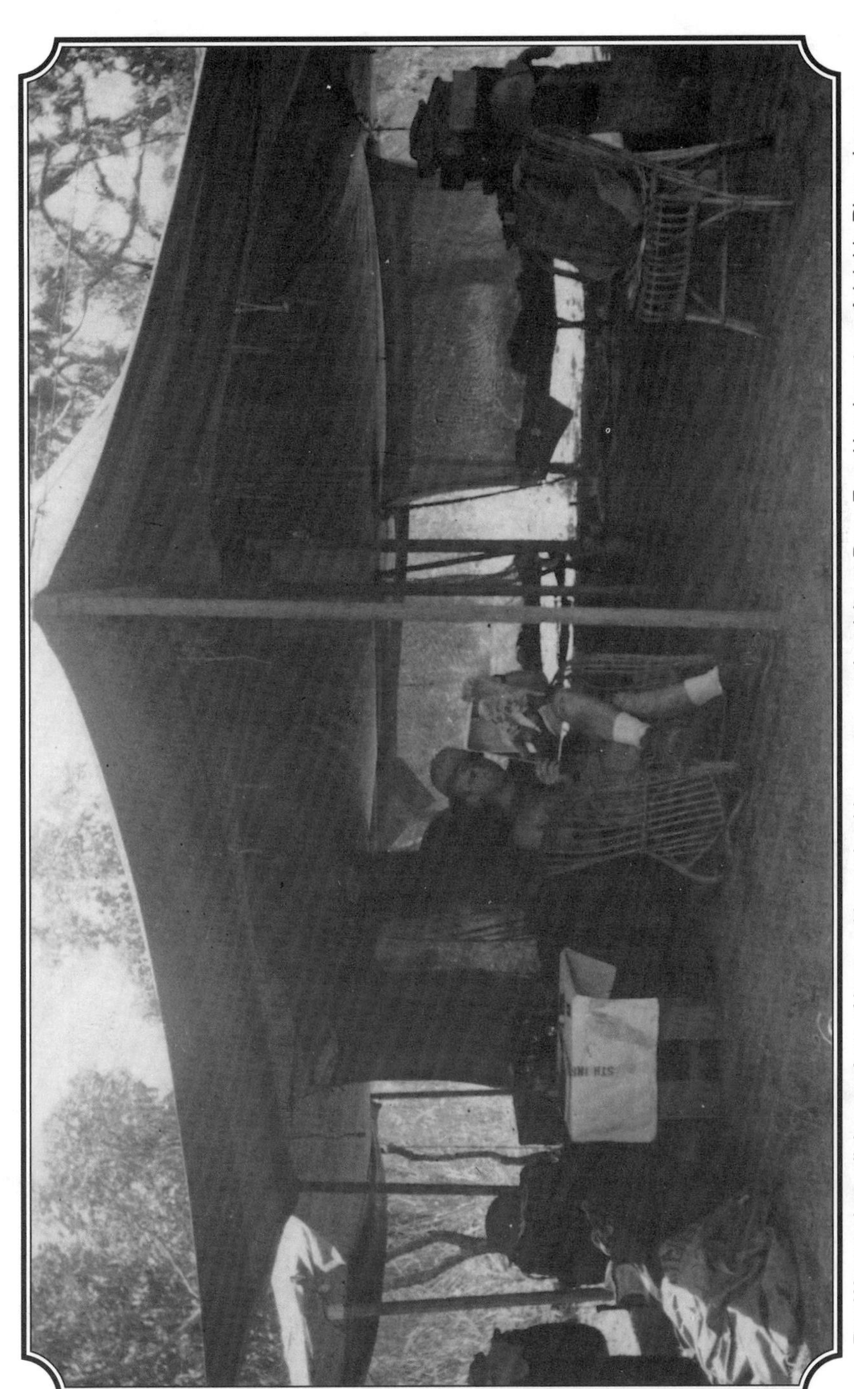

Ray Wyatt enjoys all the comforts of home without plumbing, water, or electricity at Base Four Headquarters, Adelaide River, January 1943. Two radio operators also shared the tent. The pin-up photo Wyatt is holding is of Hollywood star Veronica Lake. *Ray Wyatt photo*

The author's tent, in the kunai grass in Adelaide River, Northern Territory, February 1943. Their luggage was their A- and B-bags. Boxes, beds, and chairs stayed behind for the next soldier.
Ray Wyatt photo

An iguana tried to bite Ray Wyatt's dangling hand while he slept one afternoon in Adelaide River. *Ray Wyatt photo*

The walk-in theater with movie screen and projector in the Outback cinema at Adelaide River, February 1943.

Ray Wyatt photo

TO ALL MEMBERS
UNITED STATES ARMY FORCES
IN THE FAR EAST

WHAT TO DO IF TAKEN PRISONER OF WAR

1. **Every member of the U.S. Army whose duties place him in danger of being captured by the enemy will study a copy of this booklet.**

2. **This publication must NOT be taken into the air or into the combat zone.**

HEADQUARTERS
USAFFE

March, 1943.

PART I.

If you should be captured, give the enemy only your NAME, RANK, and SERIAL NUMBER.

You are required to give these by International Law. DON'T GIVE ANY OTHER INFORMATION.

You are a source of valuable information to the enemy, which they can use against your country, your buddies, and your family. DON'T HELP THE ENEMY !

PART II.

WHAT THE ENEMY WANTS TO KNOW.

The unit you belong to.
Its strength.
Where it is stationed.
Where other units are located.
What the recent movements of your unit have been.
Your knowledge of future movements.
Your knowledge of casualties suffered.
The types of weapons, or aircraft of your unit and—
What they can do.

1

These "instructions" were handed out to all the troops.

New details now used or to be used.

Details of armament.

Location of air bases and landing fields.

Position and technical details of Anti Aircraft and other defenses.

Past weather conditions and weather forcasts, Meteorological (weather) gauging methods.

Training methods in use at training units.

Allied tactics.

Allied knowledge of enemy tactics, plans, strength, etc.

Allied Defense Organization and raid warning system.

Home conditions—Politics—Food and clothing supplies—morale of the people and of the fighting forces.

Relations existing between Allies.

Information on these matters can be of great value to the enemy.

Do Not Help Him by answering questions.

HE IS YOUR ENEMY.

KEEP QUIET.

2

PART III.

These notes are based on fact. They are made from the experience of men who have been Prisoners of War and who have first-hand knowledge.

DIRECT QUESTIONING.

The enemy may interrogate you. If he does, DO NOT ANSWER except to give your NAME, RANK, and SERIAL NUMBER. Do not try to bluff your questioner. He is far more experienced at the game than you are. He is an expert at getting information. KEEP SILENT !

DO NOT ARGUE with him. He will outwit you.

DO NOT GIVE HIM FALSE INFORMATION. You will not succeed in misleading him, and he will punish you.

DO NOT TRY TO APPEASE HIM. If you do he will persist in questioning you for weeks and give you no respite.

DO NOT BELIEVE HIM if he tells you that another prisoner (perhaps a high

3

ranking officer) has already given information, and that there is no point in your maintaining silence.

DO NOT GIVE IN to threats. If you do he will regard you as a weakling and keep on threatening you. KEEP CALM, COLLECTED, and QUIET !

STOOL PIGEONS.

The enemy will not be satisfied with asking you direct questions. He will use stool pigeons. **Nurses** will sympathise with you and **enemy agents posing as British or Allied Prisoners of War,** will appear to befriend you.

They will get you into a conversation, show you pictures and maps, and talk about people and places you know. They will gradually proceed to talk to you about your unit, your base, your training, the location of air bases, all the time getting from you information on these matters.

You may be kept in solitary confinement for some time. It will be a great relief to talk when brought into the presence of others. DON'T DO IT !

4

OVERHEARING YOUR CONVERSATION.

The enemy will not only ask you questions and use stool pigeons, but will go to great pains to hear the things which you say when only your own friends are present. Microphones listen for him, and if you discuss anything at all with your fellow prisoners, you may be sure it will be picked up and recorded. DO NOT be led to speak because you are with men whom you know are not stool pigeons, EVEN THOUGH THEY ARE MEN THAT YOU KNEW BEFORE you were taken prisoner.

LETTERS.

REMEMBER THAT ALL OF YOUR LETTERS WILL BE CENSORED. If you write a letter do not say anything that may help the enemy to get any of the information he wants. Do not write a single word about anything that happened before you were captured. Don't address your letter to any station, company, regiment, battery, troop, battalion, regiment, squadron, wing, unit, school, A.P.O. or to any officer. Address letters to your family, using their proper home address, or to the War Department,

5

Washington, DC, to have it forwarded to your folks.

If your letter is going to be dropped over our territory DO NOT TELL where you want it to be dropped.

DOCUMENTS OR EQUIPMENT.

DON'T TAKE ANY DOCUMENTS INTO THE FIELD with you that are not absolutely necessary for the particular duty that you have to do. Search through your pockets and empty them. A single letter, a tram (street car) ticket, or a bill may let the enemy know the place you have come from and the location of your outfit.

Don't allow your equipment or personal belongings to bear trade mark tags, nor labels of your unit (outfit) or station. Don't have any marks except those prescribed on your clothing or identification tags.

While in a combat zone, or in flight, DON'T TAKE ANY NOTES on the performance or shortcomings of aircraft, armament, or equipment.

6

If you are a member of the Air Force and crash, DESTROY YOUR AIRPLANE AND MAPS BY FIRE, unless you are very sure that you are not in enemy occupied territory.

PART IV.
PROPAGANDA.

DON'T HELP ENEMY PROPAGANDA by letting yourself be talked into making a broadcast or making phonograph records.

PART V.
RIGHTS OF PRISONERS OF WAR.

Your most important rights are :

1. You are not to be compelled by force or threat of force to give any information other than your NAME, RANK, and SERIAL NUMBER.

2. You are entitled to receive letters and packages within certain limits, but only after being censored.

3. You may make complaints to the Camp Commander, and you may carry these further by asking to see a representative of the Protecting Power. However, you can

7

not say anything to him except to make your complaint. He is the representative of a neutral country agreed to by both sides appointed by international convention to ensure that prisoners of war are properly treated. In the case of prisoners in Japanese hands the Protecting Power is Switzerland.

PART VI.

1. In accordance with the custom of the Service, PAROLE MUST NOT BE GIVEN TO AN ENEMY.

2. If you succeed in escaping and in getting into friendly country, DON'T TALK about your experience with anybody. DON'T AT ANY TIME MENTION the NAME of ANYONE who helped you to escape.

3. DON'T CARRY THESE INSTRUCTIONS ON YOU OR IN AN AIRPLANE.

They are to help you and not the enemy.

BE SILENT! DON'T WEAKEN!

KEEP CALM!

8

One day in early March, orders were cut sending me to Darwin as chief operator of the Signal Corps station, and I left Adelaide River. On the way up the track, full of chuck holes and rocks, I saw my first frilled lizard. He was a cheeky fellow. When we stirred him up, he came racing across the rocky landscape with his mouth wide open and his neck frilled out ready to swallow that jeep with us in it! He had a lot of guts because he was only about two feet tall standing straight up. He came to a halt within a few feet of our jeep.

As we drove on, I saw another sight found only in Australia. Off about 50 yards from our dirt road was the home of an aboriginal family. The home was called a Mia Mia. It was a structure made of small bent-over branches of trees and covered with grass and branches. Grass had been scattered inside like that of a bird's nest.

Finally, as we approached Darwin, we drove past the Royal Australian Air Force airdrome on the north edge of town. The city was deserted. There was devastation everywhere. We soon found the only building not damaged, the Toombul Flats (apartments) near the bombed-out government buildings on the east end of the ravaged city. For the next ten months, I was in charge of a sandbagged, underground U.S. Army Signal Corps station in the bombed-out city. If the absence of normal amenities of living was amazing while we crossed the Outback, the contrast of life in beautiful Melbourne with the devastated city of Darwin was overwhelming. There were no pubs, no milk bars, no lights, and no life as usual in the ghostly rubble of what was once the "Gateway to the Orient."

The Japanese were only 450 miles away, on the island of Timor. Our only defense was a squadron of fighter planes from the U.S. 49th Fighter Group, and about 2,000 Aussie troops, some Aussie Wirraway aircraft, and some ack-ack (anti-aircraft) batteries back of our quarters, the Toombul Flats.

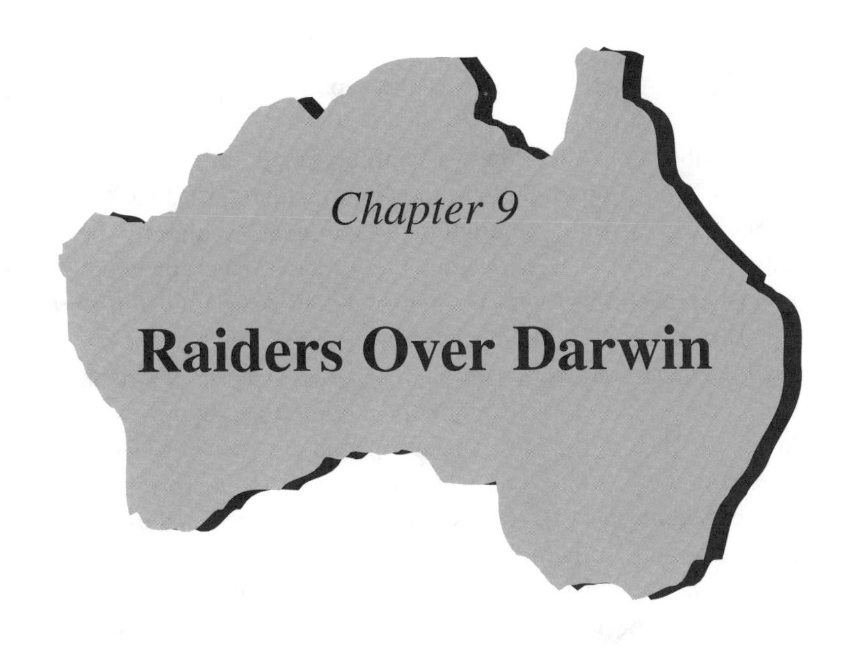

Chapter 9

Raiders Over Darwin

FOLLOWING THE FALL OF Singapore on February 15, 1942, Australia was defenseless against the superior Japanese naval forces and carrier planes that swept south through the South China Sea (and what is now Indonesia). Total defeat of the U.S. Asiatic Fleet as part of ABDA (American, British, Dutch, Australian navies) in the Battle of the Java Sea, on February 27-28, gave the Japanese complete dominance of all of the South China archipelago. America's first aircraft carrier, the USS *Langley*, perished in that battle. The Australian cruiser *Perth* lost 352 men to the seas.

The Japanese had the initiative and momentum going to establish a base of operation in northern Australia. They could have walked ashore on Mindil or Fannie Bay beaches in Darwin with only slight resistance from local Australian troops and shore batteries.

Before the Japanese attack on Pearl Harbor, American bombers and fighter planes had been sent to bolster the British defenses in the South China Sea in an effort to prevent the Japanese from taking the Dutch East Indies. But it was too little too late. They became part of 100,000 Allied casualties as the Japanese juggernaut rolled over them.

On November 27, 1941, "the war-warning telegram" had been sent by the War and Navy Departments to the Commanders in Hawaii. And thus the defense of Australia, though not "planned," indirectly began on November 30, 1941, a week before the United States declared war on Japan on December 8th. A convoy, consisting of seven U.S. transports and cargo vessels escorted by the heavy cruiser *Pensacola* and the submarine chaser *Niagara*, set out for Australia. The convoy put in at Brisbane Harbor on December 22, 1941. Originally intended as support for General MacArthur in the Philippines, the troop convoy then left Brisbane for Manila during the last days of December by way of the Torres Straits and the Arafura Sea north of Darwin. On learning that the Japanese had taken Sumatra, Java, and Borneo, the ships were ordered into the big harbor at Darwin on January 6, 1942. Japanese forces landed on Timor, in the eastern end of the Netherlands East Indies, by the middle of February. Allied ships lay at anchor in Darwin's harbor, approximately 450 miles from the island of Timor. On February 14th, Australian and American ships, including some of the *Pensacola* convoy, attempted to land troops on Timor to counter the Japanese. After surviving a concerted attack by a superior number of Japanese fighters and bombers, all the Allied ships managed to steam back to Port Darwin harbor.

On February 18 three U.S. ships — *Tulagi, Port Mar*, and *Mauna Loa* — and an Australian ship, HMAS *Meigs,* began unloading troops at the Darwin docks on the east end of the city. By sundown the *Meigs* and the *Mauna Loa* had finished unloading the troops, and the two other U.S. vessels, loaded with American servicemen, waited in the harbor. Two British cargo ships, *Neptuna* and *Zealandia,* loaded with munitions, were also alongside the main wharf ready for unloading.

At 9:58 a.m. the next morning, 188 Japanese bombers and fighter planes from aircraft carriers of the Nagumo Task Force — the *Akagi, Soryo, Zuikaku, Shokaku*, and *Hiryu* — the same carrier force that had bombed Pearl Harbor 2½ months earlier, leveled the docks and the city of Darwin and sank or damaged 12 ships of some 45 in the big harbor. Two hours later a second force of 54 land-based enemy planes completed the total devastation of the city.

Ships in the harbor and the RAAF airdrome suffered major damage. Some 240 Australians and Americans were killed and 300 to 400 were injured. Of 120 crewmen on the USS *Peary,* 85 went down to a watery grave in the harbor. The attack left Australia with no effective naval force or air defense to combat the free-wheeling Japanese.

February 19, 1942, will live in infamy for Australia; some called it a second Pearl Harbor.

With complete dominance of all the South Seas and superior numbers of aircraft and troops, the question as to why the Japanese did not continue their drive for Australia was debated for years after the war.

"Scottie" Mohr, a civilian employee of QANTAS (Queensland and Northern Territory Air Service) in Darwin, the halfway point between Sydney and Hong Kong, survived that first raid. He told me of dock workers on strike that morning who were caught in the raid, while they were sitting on the eastern slopes of the bluff that overlooks the main wharf where the *Neptuna* lay at anchor. Others had joined the exodus down the track toward Alice Springs and Mount Isa the morning of the raid.

Air defense for the little metropolis of Darwin at the time of the February 19th raid consisted of 11 single-engine Curtiss P-40 Kittyhawk fighters flown by the U.S. 49th Fighter Group, a squadron of Consolidated Catalina Flying Boats of U.S. Navy Patrol Wing 10 stationed at Melville Island north of Darwin, and a few Australian Wirraways — locally built and resembling the AT-6 Harvard — used for training purposes. During the first raid on Darwin, the 49th lost all its aircraft except for one being repaired on the ground. None of the Catalina Flying Boats survived. The situation looked hopeless for the defense of Australia and an Allied holding action at Darwin.

Before the withdrawal of the remaining 49th Fighter Group from Darwin, the Australian government in August 1942 asked Great Britain for fighter planes. In February 1943, one year after Japanese raiders had completely destroyed the defenseless city, 100 British Spitfires — Mark VC fighter planes — were delivered to the east coast of Australia for assemblage and training duty. The Spitfire was known for its superiority in the skies over Europe during the summer of 1940 in the Battle of Britain. It had a Rolls-Royce Merlin 1,470-hp engine, with a three-bladed propeller, capable of generating a speed of 370 mph.

According to Michael Burns, in *Spitfire! Spitfire!*, three squadrons of the aircraft were formed into the No. 1 Fighter Wing RAAF, sometimes known as the Churchill Wing. RAAF Squadrons No. 452 and No. 457, and RAF Squadron No. 54 were first sent to Batchelor Field, 120 miles south of Darwin, for relocation to bush airbases. No. 452 was subsequently based at Strauss Field, 60 miles south of Darwin; No. 457 was located at Livingstone Field, near Darwin; and No. 54 was at the RAAF airdrome in Darwin. The Spitfires were led by Wing Commander Clive "Killer" Caldwell, Australia's outstanding fighter pilot who had already recorded 29 victories in the European Theater.

The entire country of Australia — as well as Allied troops, especially Australian and U.S. air forces personnel in the Northern Territory — breathed a sigh of relief with the arrival of the Spitfires. Some evenings in Darwin, as the Spitfire pilots changed shifts, we watched these sleek planes go nearly straight up in a intriguing spiraling maneuver. It was a practice called "follow-the-leader," testing not only a pilot's skill but his courage before being forced to peel out of the ever-tightening spiral. We called it "chicken out" in the States; Australians called it, "A bloody good show. My oath!"

The three Spitfire squadrons in the Northern Territory were readied to meet the Japanese Mitsubishi A6M Zero, Japan's main weapon in the air war in the Southwest Pacific Theater. With a reported air speed of 358 mph, the Zero was thought to be no match for the faster Spitfire, which was supposed to be a surprise to the Japanese. All the preparation was prelude to the "Spitfire versus Zero show" in the Southwest Pacific.

After No. 54 Spitfire Squadron had settled in, Ray "Vandy" Vanderpool, another radio operator, and I climbed into the jeep and traveled out to the RAAF airdrome to see these super machines. When we drove onto the base, we saw 12 beautiful, impressive-looking aircraft lined up in perfect formation under tall eucalyptus trees and shrubs on the edge of the runway. We stopped the jeep near a group of men and just looked at the planes. Seeing we were Americans, one fellow in a jumpsuit walked over and offered his hand, asking if we were stationed there. "You're with the Army, aren't you?" he asked.

We told him we operated the Army Signal Corps station in Darwin. "We give the air raid warnings when you guys take off from here."

After exchanging greetings and hometown information, we discovered that the pilot was from Oakland, California. Early in the war he had gone to England to become a part of an American Eagle squadron flying

Spitfires in defense of Great Britain. Later, he had become part of the 54th Squadron.

He pointed up and remarked, "There's sure a lot of sky up here."

Lots of room for dogfights, I thought. We turned to leave as we told him we hoped to see him up there, and holding up my pocket-size Kodak Brownie camera, I asked if I could take his picture by one of the Spitfires.

We walked over to one of the planes and took several exposures. Then we visited until he had to report back to his group. Vandy and I drove back to our quarters in time for evening chow.

A few weeks later, I returned to the airdrome where I saw war in its most gruesome form. On a clear morning, as I was coming off the midnight shift, a plane was reported to have crashed at an RAAF field about four miles north of town. Vandy and I took off to see what had happened and were among the first to drive down the runway through the wreckage scattered over a 100-yard area. The largest pieces of debris were the motors; the rest were small and unidentifiable. We stopped near an Australian aircraft maintenance man who said it had been a two-motored Australian Beaufighter.

Light smoke hung over the wreckage, and I could smell an odor of burnt oil and grease. As I stepped out of the jeep to survey the total scene, for some reason I looked down at my feet. There I saw a shiny leather boot with bloody flesh and bone sticking out of it. I lost control and wretched in my hand. Then I noticed two men putting body parts into a sack. I quickly got back into the jeep and moved away from the site.

We learned later that it was an Australian pilot whose plane had caught its tailwheel on the top of a eucalyptus tree at full throttle. There was no chance for survival.

Before the runway was completely cleared, Spitfires were engaged in their first major encounter with the Japanese. On the afternoon of April 15th, 14 Japanese bombers and their fighter escort came in high over the Timor Sea bent on destroying Darwin's oil tanks and the airdrome. "She's on," a typical Aussie expression for any kind of action, was heard from the Australian 3.7 anti-aircraft battery stationed right behind our quarters. Spitfires took to the air trying to gain sufficient altitude to contest the Zeros flying cover above the bombers. In that first encounter, the Japanese were not surprised. In his book, Michael Burns reported that the Spitfires lost four planes while destroying seven Japanese planes in that first meeting. The squadrons needed to focus more on their procedures.

A radar station on Bathurst Island north of Darwin had given the Spitfire squadron approximately 45 minutes to assemble and climb above 25,000 feet to meet the Japanese fighter escort. But with the sun behind them as they approached Darwin from the west, the Japanese Zeros had the advantage. Their pilots could locate the shiny Spitfires easily, whereas Spitfire pilots had difficulty seeing the Zeros and getting above them for their attack. Though faster than the Zeros, the Spitfires needed to attain altitude rapidly and be prepared to "bounce" off the top of the enemy fighters before attacking the Japanese "Betty" Mitsubishi bombers. This maneuver was not always easy, because the pilots had to get extra boost out of the planes' engines after takeoff.

After a lackluster first meeting with the Japanese, the Spitfires began to suffer from Australia's tropical climate and the strain on the Merlin engines. More planes were lost to mechanical problems than to combat casualties. Newspaper accounts were unduly critical and expressed disappointment in the Spitfires' performances. After a major encounter with the Zeros over the skies of Darwin, the integrity and the capability of the Spitfires began to concern even the troops on the ground.

To supplement the squadrons in the forward action, two more squadrons, Nos. 548 and 549, were sent to the Northern Territory to protect Darwin's oil supplies and harbor installations. A total of 247 Spitfire Mark VC's arrived in Australia for the No. 1 Fighter Wing.

In the few months following the first raid, Australian and American forces poured an unimaginable amount of equipment and personnel into the Northern Territory. Despite muddy roads and miles of quagmires, in one year over 50 air bases and supply depots were built on the north-south track, as well as the Barkly Highway to Mount Isa and Townsville. An estimated 200,000 Allied soldiers, including Australian, American, Canadian, and Dutch, traversed the Northern Territory during the war. The major effort was to get the big bombers in the air to strike Japanese bases in the South Seas and the waters back toward the Philippine Islands.

As early as August 1942, Allied Consolidated B-24 Liberators and Lockheed Hudson bombers had begun flying from bases in the Northern Territory on some of the longest missions ever attempted in the South Pacific. Ten crew members of a 380th Bombardment Group B-24, affectionally called *Shady Lady* and piloted by Lieutenant Doug Craig, flew 2,300 nautical miles on August 13th to Balikpapan, Borneo, as part of a squadron of 12 bombers. All made it back except *Shady Lady*, who ran out of fuel, and Lieutenant Craig had to ditch the big Liberator in a swamp along the coast south of Darwin. American GIs subsequently unloaded the plane and cleared a path through the jungle, and in an unbelievable bit of maneuvering, Major Zed Smith and Sergeant Marshall of the 528th Squadron took the plane out of the swamp to Fenton Field near Darwin.

Additional Spitfires were needed for fighter coverage for the increasing number of Allied bomber raids into Dutch East Indies, as they continued to carry the war to the Japanese.

Back at Darwin, Japanese bombers normally flew at altitudes over 25,000 feet and tried to stay above the range of the Australian ack-ack guns. The main objective of the battery next to our radio station was to get in a record number of shots during each raid, and put flak among Japanese bombers most of the time before their bombs could be released.

Because of their inaccuracy, Japanese bombing runs were always worrisome to those in the target area. The Japanese bombers depended on the lead bombardier for a signal to release the load. This resulted in a scattered pattern over the target. And thus even though you were not in the target area, you could still get hit — not a good feeling, adding to the problem of where to go to avoid annihilation. In contrast, the Americans used the Norden bombsight, a special precision instrument for pinpoint accuracy on specific targets. During these Japanese air raids, all one could do was to hunker down and take whatever happened. I recall looking up from my trench and seeing 15 or 18 two-motored Japanese bombers flying in a tight V formation headed for our area.

During my time in Darwin I kept a diary and a journal. I wanted a record of what it was like to be in a war, in life-threatening situations. It would serve as proof of the action, which could be checked for accuracy later if need be. Many times after major raids, I wrote of the events as I experienced them. Some of these descriptions follow unedited from my diary and journals. The "ZZZ" I speak of was actually the Morse Code signal for the letter "Z," which when repeated — ZZZ — was the warning for an air raid. Air-raid "Yellow" was an alert that meant enemy planes were about ten minutes away. Air-raid "Red" meant "take cover."

Diary — Sunday May 2, 1943:

To work at 8:30. No church. Air raid at 10:10. Gave the ZZZ & air raid Yellow to all. Got in trench. Saw them come over. 18 of them. Dropped their eggs & left. Spitfires not in sight. All over at 10:50. Hit the RAAF airdrome (Hell's Corner). Sent several messages. Played basketball at night. Worked till 8:00. In bed at 9:00.

And from my journal:

RAIDERS OVER DARWIN

May 2, 1943

The Sunday after Easter, May 2, I was on duty in our dugout radio station in Darwin, Australia. It was a nice morning with a few cirrus clouds starting to push across the western horizon over the Timor Sea. There was no traffic on our radio network. I was alone in the radio room most of the time. The other seven guys were either talking, sleeping, or riding around the area. At 11:30 the 12-drop switchboard rang. I answered with, "U.S. Army Switchboard — Darwin." The reply was, "Air Raid Yellow," from the Australian Army operator out at Larrakeyah Barracks. Since things were so quiet it startled me, though we could expect Tojo over any time. I heard the ships in the harbor sound the alarm as they pulled out into the harbor. With my vibroplex I transmitted ZZZ to stations on our U.S. network. Then I stepped out and yelled, "Air raid Yellow," to guys in the area. They answered me, casually got their helmets, and strolled over to the slit trenches in front of our quarters. My trench buddy Pokoi, from Chicago, ran over to the nearby Australian ack-ack battery and looked at their radar scanner. It showed planes headed toward Darwin. Pokoi came back sputtering, "Nearly 50 Jap planes are coming in!"

After giving the air raid signal I put on my helmet and headed out to the trench that we had dug previously. I was going to take my chances in the trench rather than in the sandbagged dugout for fear of its collapsing on me. The fellows outside the trenches were arguing over the wisest place to be considering the number of planes Pokoi had reported. Some wanted to go to the beach a mile and a half away because the Australian ack-ack battery, only about 30 yards from our trenches, was a likely target if we stayed where we were. The others said they would feel safer in the trenches because the beach had Australian troops stationed nearby.

Then everyone ran for the trenches. Pokoi jumped in beside me holding his helmet, gas mask, and a little 2" X 3" green Bible in his hand. He was extremely nervous and drenched with sweat. When I looked up I saw 18 two-motored, Mitsubishi bombers in a crowded "V" formation flying at about 25,000 feet and headed right for us. When I saw they were nearing the point for releasing their bombs, I kept my head low and watched with open mouth. The Aussie ack-ack battery opened up right behind us. I thought Japanese bombs had landed near us. The first ack-ack burst caused little pebbles to bounce on the ground by our trench. I spat out a mouthful of dirt and rocks. Then I heard Pokoi squealing like a pig caught under a gate. He screamed, ". . . I'm hit! I'm hit!" I looked and saw that a 3-inch sliver of a sunbaked rock had fallen against the back of his leg. I said, "Awh. Fer God sake! Pokoi. It's just a rock. You'll probably get a purple heart."

Our Australian ack-ack fire was a little off target and several batteries were in on it now. One burst scored a hit and a plane on the left wing of the formation of bombers began to wobble and lose altitude. The Jap bombers went up a few thousand feet, then dropped their loads. We heard them whistling and growing louder as they neared the ground. That's when I was really scared. In that brief interval I know Pokoi read that Bible twice. Some of the leaves were wrinkled from his sweat and wet fingers. Most of the bombs landed near the oil tanks a block away from us. Then the Jap bombers circled and headed back out to sea with two Zeros trailing behind them daring anyone to chase them. Our Spitfires (British Mark IV) were busy chasing some other Zeros back toward Timor. We watched, then slowly began to emerge from our trenches, digging out the cigarettes. We could see the smoke and dust rising from the docks and oil storage area. Nothing had come close to us. The Japanese bombers' objective had been the wharf, docks and some oil storage tanks east of our location. Two of the GIs jumped into the jeep and drove around to see the damage. I went back to radio room and in about fifteen minutes the "All Clear" signal was sounded by a ship in the harbor. Our Commanding Officer called in a message to be transmitted "Priority." It read: "Eighteen enemy bombers and thirty fighters raided Darwin at 11:30 AM. Explosive and anti-personnel bombs were dropped. Damage and losses undetermined. No U.S. casualties. Complete report will follow." The Japs had come and gone again.

Diary — Sunday, June 20:

No church. Slept 'till about 10:30. Lying awake I heard the Air Raid warning. Got dressed & made for trench. First we saw the Zeros zipping around. Then the formation of bombers. Saw 6 Spitfires dive on them and then break formation. Good ack-ack today. And some real dog-fighting. Sky full of planes. Explosions. Smoke. A lone dive bomber dropped bombs. More smoke. Dog fights. Into jeep and out to see damage. Several wounded mostly from anti-personnel bombs. Hit water pipe. Ruined our telephone lines. Couple trucks on fire. Running around all afternoon looking at holes. Pilot's oxygen truck hit. Ate supper. Saw show. Went to bed.

From my journal:

AIR RAID YELLOW

. . . At about 10:30 Sunday morning, June 20, I was awakened by a Signal Corps operator shouting, "Air raid Yellow!" I wasn't exactly asleep because somehow I expected a raid this morning. The Liberty ship USS Hall Young had been unloading at the docks, and "Washing Machine Charlie" had been over the day before reconnoitering. When someone hollered "air raid," I felt it would be the real thing. The Japs usually bombed us on Sundays.

I heard the ships in the harbor whistle, and I knew they were pulling out into open water to get away from the target area . . . usually the docks and the oil storage tanks nearby. I took my time dressing and went down to our radio room for my helmet. All of our guys were around and we had sent the air raid alert. Some were already in their trench, and others wandered around looking up at the sky over the Indian Ocean to the west. As I sat on the edge of my trench I could hear lots of planes in the air. Spitfires had been up for about 10 minutes and were going out to sea to try to bust-up the Jap formation as they came in toward us.

Suddenly the defense guns opened up all around the harbor. We hit the trenches pronto. Then we noticed three planes diving out of the white clouds overhead almost straight up above us. It looked like a dull start, and I wondered if it was a fair dinkum raid. The Jap fighters usually come in and have a go at us first. The ack-ack guns ceased for awhile, yet we could hear aircraft all around us. In and out of the clouds we could see fighters but we couldn't tell who was chasing whom. Some 40 millimeter cannons were being fired in the harbor area. Suddenly we heard the swish and high-pitched whine of an airplane falling right above us at about 2,000 feet altitude. Headed toward the RAAF air drome north of town was a Spitfire plane with its propeller shot off. The poor guy was on a dead stick. His only hope was to hold enough altitude to reach the landing field. We learned later an American gun crew aboard the new Liberty ship had mistaken him for a Zero and had given him a burst right in his motor. Then over the west end of Darwin above Myilly Point some real action going on was over the Timor Sea where about twenty planes were in several dogfights. Planes were diving everywhere. Over to one side Spitfires were diving into a formation of sixteen Mitsubishi "Betty" bombers heading right for us. One bomber pulled out of formation smoking as Spitfires followed him. The bombers came on toward their target. Next out of the clouds came six Spitfires diving in the formation again. At first I thought it was a plane falling, then I saw others diving right behind the leader. They were about 2 miles out now and the view was first class. Another Jap bomber left the formation and headed back toward Timor with two Spitfires on his tail. As soon as the last Spitfire dived through, the Aussie ack-ack opened up and did a terrific job. All of their bursts were right in there. Smoke began pouring from the engines of 2 Japanese bombers. Striving for altitude they came on in, then dropped their loads and headed back to Timor or the Celebes Islands. Dogfights were so thick we couldn't follow all of them. I saw two different fights right above me as well as farther back from the original big brawl out over the harbor. To our left a formation of 12 Japanese twin-motored "Betty" bombers came in very low strafing and dropping 50 lb. anti-personnel bombs. Luckily just this morning most of the Air Force equipment taken from the new ship in the harbor had been moved out and was on its way to some of the many air bases south of Darwin.

During a lull in the action we saw Jap bombers coming in again. Bombs were exploding everywhere and black smoke billowed skyward. It was sort of potluck with bombers coming in from different angles. I watched a lone bomber coming in over RAAF field out near the Wallaby dumps. I saw him drop his bombs and zoom on out. Smoke soon rose from that area. The dogfights died down and only an occasional chase was going on. Slowly one by one the Spitfires came in and landed at their base on the north side of town. We sat for awhile on the edge of our trenches waiting for the "All Clear" signal from the ships in the harbor.

Vandy and I jumped into a jeep and headed out to see the damage. On the road out near the civilian airdrome we passed two ambulances carrying in the wounded. When we came to the RAAF Field where I had seen the one lone bomber drop his bombs, we noticed that a bomb had landed in the bush and started another bush fire. On our way to the "dumps" we could see where the anti-personnel bombs had been dropped along the highway near a Bofor gun position. [At the time, the Swedish Bofor was a new, quick-firing 40mm anti-aircraft gun.] On arriving at Wallaby Dumps we saw more damage. Telephone lines Vandy and I had hung on some trees this morning for the Air Force were in a tangled mess for about six sections of poles. A US Air Force truck was burning and water was running over the road. Bombs had hit the water pipes supplying the city. A small building was scattered all over the area. A freight car loaded with barrels of oil and petrols was blazing and made the scene look really dramatic. Three small trucks and the Air Force's big semi-trailer containing oxygen-generating equipment were full of holes. We rode around some shell craters picking up pieces of shrapnel and looking for Japanese bombs that had exploded. Their detonation points had Japanese writing on them and made choice souvenirs. There were not many casualties, but we wondered how the communique could get around all this damage. It was luck that the Air Force had taken most of their equipment south earlier this morning. Too bad they hadn't taken that semi with the oxygen-generator with them. Tojo had come and gone again. The Australians were saying, as they had said before, "Every time the bloody Yanks come to town the Japs come over. Wouldn't it?" (Wouldn't it ruin your future?).

The day before the June 20 raid we had received a call from some U.S. Army Air Forces guys wanting phones installed in their camp north of town. They were in a thicket of trees, I think, near Four-Mile, and well camouflaged — or so we thought. Because they appeared to be new to the Darwin area, we told them about the air raid "Yellow" and "Red" alarm system.

We hung several phones in Army-style satchels at a command post and near several trenches. The next day when Vandy and I went looking at the damage, we saw evidence that the Japanese bombers had dropped anti-personnel bombs on the campsite. These bombs would weigh from 35 to 50 pounds, loaded with small pieces of sharp objects. The bomb would burst on impact and expel bits and pieces at about 18 inches above the ground. They were called "daisy cutters" and could shred a small sapling or post 20 to 30 feet away. Though I never saw the contents, these bombs supposedly had razor blades, small nuts and bolts, and scrap metal of all kinds in them. I remember the scrap-metal we had collected before the war for Japan, who was buying it from America to make steel. I was still a teenager back in Kansas, and especially recall a pile we had collected beside the barn on the farm we moved to following the foreclosure of our original farmstead east of Effingham. Ironically, we were getting some of it back in a highly concentrated manner.

One of the phones we went out to retrieve after the raid was pretty well torn and scratched, as if it might have sustained damage from a daisy cutter. Two wounded soldiers taken from a trench below one of the phones were nearly severed at the waist. We were told they had decided to sit on the edge of their trench and watch the show, not knowing what an anti-personnel shell could do.

Diary — Monday June 28:

Monday. Up at 8:00 & ate breakfast. Then Vandy and I started putting in our lines to Vesties [our commercial meat-supply warehouse]. At 10:00 Air Raid. We went to the beach. They, 9 bombers, dropped bombs right near us. Really scared me & dog. Dropped within 50 yds. Dust & sand flying. Saw one hit the water. Back to work all afternoon on line. Took first hot shower at Scotties. In bed at 9:30.

From my journal:

AIR RAID ON DARWIN

June 28, '43

Monday was a nice clear morning in Darwin. I could sense a raid was coming. Birds and hawks were circling around. There was something in the air. At 9:30 while putting in telephone lines out to Vestey's Meatworks I mentioned to "Vandy" Vanderpool . . . we might have a raid. At 10:30 we came to the end of our spool of wire and started back to our quarters at T [Toombul] Flats on the east end of Darwin on Cavanagh Street.

At about 10:30 I saw a squadron of Spitfires go up and thought there must be a raid on. Sure enough the Aussie ack-ack reported they were plotting 15 planes coming in at 18,000 feet. They were still about 5 minutes out. Ships in the harbor began sounding the alarm and another raid was on.

Taking my time I sent the air raid warning ZZZ to our signal quarters at Adelaide River and other stations on our northern Australia network. Getting into a jeep I drove down to the Mindil Beach about 2 miles away. We had dug an extra trench under some palm trees along the beach above high tide level. Our lieutenant and everyone else from our station were there already. Two nights previous I had picked up Tokyo Rose on the Hallicrafter receiver. During her late night broadcast she had told us the Japanese were going to wipe Darwin off the map and for us to save ourselves and get out.

Sirens began blowing from several points again. After about 5 minutes we heard the unforgettable drone of Japanese bombers.

There were a lot of them coming in from every direction. It was eerie. I thought of what Tokyo Rose had said last night.

Six of us and a small dog ran down into our trench made of corrugated roofing and bags of sand banked up against the sides. Our trench was about 5 feet deep and had one end open for our entry. The roar of planes grew louder and then we saw 9 Japanese Zeros flying over our site. Soon we saw Japanese bombers in perfect formation right above us. The Ack-Ack guns opened up and were putting some flack in around them. We hunkered down into the trench. I heard the first bunch of bombs coming down and then the explosions. I peeked out and saw smoke and dirt rising from Bullocky Point right across from us on the point of the beach. Big geysers of water shot skyward and it looked like the whole end of the Point was going up. A big search light was on that point. One bomb landed on the beach a ways down from us. Then came a sharp whistling noise and I put my head down again.

Bombs were walking closer down the beach toward us and I was really scared. I began to feel smothered in the trench . . . a kind of claustrophobia. The little dog squeezed in between my legs began whimpering. His nose began bleeding from banging his head against the corrugated side of the trench. I didn't look out anymore. I was sure the bombs were landing right outside our trench. They were 500 pounders. I didn't know what to do and thought of praying between the impact of the bombs. My back felt as broad as a football field. Funny how cock-sure I was and unconcerned until bombs began shaking the ground around us. One of the new guys sent up from Headquarters last week was standing up outside the trench with his hands folded looking at the sky. Afterwards we asked him why. He said he was waiting for the bombs to whistle. "If you don't hear them whistling, it's too late," he said. "If you can still hear them, then you are okay." He had been reading too many thrill magazines from the states. Just at that moment a bomb exploded shaking the ground around the trench and showering us with sand. The next one would be right on us. It never came! Gad! I will never forget that moment.

When I was sure they had all dropped, I crawled out of the trench and looked around. The dust along the beach and under the palm trees was slowly drifting out to sea. Even with all those bombs the Japs missed Vestey's warehouse farther up the beach from us. The wind had carried the bombs a little off target. They had scattered bombs for half of a mile up and down the beach. An ambulance pulled up and a bunch of men gathered around a crater. Then the ambulance pulled away. It must have been Australian soldiers. None of our guys were missing. I walked over to our jeep which was back aways from the beach. Water was leaking from the radiator where shrapnel had made several holes in it. I began feeling my legs and stomach wondering if I was leaking blood. Like that jeep I could be out of action, too.

A dogfight between a Zero and a Spitfire was going on right above us as several other Zeros sped across the sky going west toward Timor and Sumatra trying to catch up with the bombers circling back out to the sea. Soon the bombers left and one by one the Spitfires came gliding in to the RAAF airdrome. When the "ALL CLEAR" sounded we walked away from the trench, got into the jeep, and despite a hot radiator made it back to our quarters. There were some good sized craters around the telephone lines we had strung to Bullocky Point only yesterday. Most of the bombs had landed between the Vestey's Meatworks and Mindil Beach where we had been.

We drove out to Dudley Point where smoke was boiling skyward. Not much damage considering all the action. Three Australian soldiers were reported injured. I waited for the Captain's report so I could begin encoding a message to Base Section One HQS.

Air raids on Darwin and the Allied airbases in the Northern Territory were usually during daylight hours, but sometimes the Japanese used moonlit nights as a harassment tactic to keep everyone on edge. The Japanese played with Darwin like a cat might play with a wounded mouse. During one full week they sent just one or two planes over every three or four hours.

During a July raid, with about 50 Japanese planes coming in on us, only seven Spitfires managed to challenge the raiders. Spitfires in that raid either were grounded or turned back because of engine problems. One of the early tricks the Japanese pilots pulled on the Spitfires was to entice them to follow them too far out to sea. During some of the earlier raids, a few Spitfire pilots had to ditch their plane because of emptied fuel tanks.

The record of the Spitfires bothered everyone and was the subject of many of the bull sessions that were part of everyday Army life.

One moonlit night a convoy of eight trucks loaded with ammunition parked in an esplanade about 100 yards south of our headquarters and not far from the old Hotel Darwin. They were hauling ammunition to air bases down the track. I walked over to see who they were and to instruct them what to do in case of an air raid, and learned they were a transport group new to the Northern Territory and on their first trip into Darwin. I told them that if there was a raid to leave their bomb-loaded trucks and to high-tail it for the beach about 100 yards away. They would have to take the winding path down the steep cliff to get to the beach to safety.

As predicted, the Japanese bombers and fighter escort made their usual run over Darwin during the night. When I checked the next morning to see if the truckers were OK, the men were in a state of shock and milling around a body. One of their drivers had gone over the cliff. When he had heard the ships in the harbor blowing the air raid warning and saw the bombers overhead, he didn't take the trail as instructed. His body was found on the beach below. The new transport group learned that bombs were not the only mortal hazard in Darwin.

The war waged on and monotony and fatigue began to affect everyone. November weather was nice, but the monsoon season was about to begin. I had survived some 30 raids, and I began to have sleepless nights and nightmares, wondering how long I could be so lucky.

Chapter 10

Darwin, Australia

ONCE CALLED THE "Gateway to the Orient," Darwin was a tropical city on Australia's northwest tip before the Japanese had completely obliterated it on February 19, 1942. Isolated by 2,000 miles of desert and bush from the country's trade centers along the east coast, its economic survival depended a great deal on commerce with the islands of Dutch East Indies and the China Coast to the west in Indonesia. With a good harbor and two airdromes, this isolated outpost was of strategic importance to Japan as well as to Allied forces during World War II.

An important service base for Queensland and Northern Territory Aerial Services, Darwin had attracted international attention when Amelia Earhart and Fred Noonan set down their two-motored Lockheed Electra at Darwin's airdrome for refueling before flying over the Owen Stanley Mountains to Lae, New Guinea, where on July 2, 1937, they began their ill-fated flight toward Howland Island in the Central Pacific. (There are various theories regarding their fatal trip. Some believe that because of what Earhart and Noonan saw of Japanese installations and military build-up at Lae and the Markham

Taxis were replaced by a jeep in Darwin following the Japanese raid on February 19, 1942. *Ray Wyatt photo*

Valley of New Guinea, as well as all of the South Seas in 1937, Japanese warlords could not let the two survive to tell their story in the United States. The Japanese made sure they were there to pick up Earhart and Noonan when their plane went down following their distress calls to U.S. ships in the area of Howland Island.)

Just before the war, Darwin's population was approximately 5,000, according to Ernestine Hill who described Darwin and the Northern Territory, as well as all of Australia in *Australian Frontier*. Her book was specifically published in 1942 for use by the United States Armed Forces in Australia. I found a copy in the ruins of the American Headquarters building on Cavanagh Street in Darwin.

According to Hill, Darwin's population at the turn of the century had consisted of 1,000 British, 600 Australian-born Chinese, 100 Japanese, and 200 to 300 total of Swedes, Slavs, Swiss, Greeks, Maoris, Maltese, Malayas, Manilamen, Siamese, Cingalese, Samoans, Portugese, and a few Afghans and African Negros. Hill wrote of a mixture of "black and white, black and yellow Chinese-Greek, Chilean-aborigine, Cingalese-white-

The American Headquarters was destroyed by a direct hit from a Japanese dive-bomber during the raid on Darwin in 1942. *Ray Wyatt photo*

Toombul Flats was the Americans' second Headquarters in Darwin. Note the oil tanks on the left, a favorite target of Japanese bombers and fighter planes. *Ray Wyatt photo*

Many homes in Darwin were built on stilts for "air conditioning." Note the louvered siding for ventilation. Very few were left standing after the February Japanese attack. Most were brought down by concussion from bombs.

Commonwealth of Australia, Department of Information photo aborigine, Malay-Kanaka-Greek-aborigine, double half-castes, quadroons, octoroons with red hair and freckles, and Japanese-German" all living in one square-mile. Their assimilation made Darwin a fascinating place before the war. And governing the admixtures of culture was a challenge for Australia's officials, whose payroll made up most of the city's economic base.

With its face toward China and its back to the giant Australian bush, Darwin was truly a polyglot of cultures surviving on shipping, pearling, and livestock production. However, by 1940, the population had dropped to near 3,000, including native aborigines within the city limits. Then, with the influx of military personnel, and workers constructing oil tanks and harbor facilities for military preparedness, the city quickly grew to 5,000 and had a healthy economy prior to the Japanese conquest of the South China Seas.

Before the first raid on February 19, 1942, nearly all the women and children in Darwin were evacuated by ship or railway, or on the one dirt highway going south through the interior of Australia. Australian soldiers stationed at Larrakeyah Barracks on Myilly Point, along with a few government employees, maintained the city's hospital and airdromes after the raid. Looting and disrepair reduced the city to a desolate village. Less than 15 civilians — mostly government officials — remained during the first year or so after the city was evacuated.

After his arrival on March 17, General Douglas MacArthur had stated that Australia was not prepared to fight a war on its own soil. According to Geoffery Perrot, in *There's a War to be Won*, the inefficient railroad, inadequate communication facilities, and overloaded utilities were only a few immediate considerations. Australia was practically defenseless at home in 1942 with its 6th, 7th, and 9th Divisions in the western desert of North Africa and its 8th Division taken as prisoners of war of the Japanese in Singapore.

Monsoons, thousands of miles of muddy dirt road, inadequate water supplies, and scarce machinery often prevented supplies of any kind from reaching Darwin, even in peacetime. Nearly all of the Allies' equipment and armed forces were still on Australia's east coast in the early part of 1942. Darwin was vulnerable to the onrushing Japanese, but fate intervened in the form of a mix-up in strategy by Japan's army and naval commanders in Tokyo.

Japan decided to ignore Darwin and concentrated its efforts on taking

Port Moresby and Rabaul, in New Guinea, and Guadalcanal in the Solomon Islands, hoping to isolate Australia from U.S. supply lines pouring men and machines into the South Pacific Theater of war. Australia's Top End, which had once flourished from mining, pearling, shipping, and some of the world's largest cattle stations, thus became a military post of over 100,000 men and encompassed some 10,000 square miles of bush accessible by only the one mostly dirt road and the Coral and Arafura seas.

As chief operator of Advanced Headquarter's Signal Station, I was responsible for sending air raid warnings to other stations in Base Section One. It was sometimes difficult to know when to send them. The Japanese had spotters on Timor, 450 miles west of Darwin, who began counting Allied planes on their outbound missions to Japanese bases in the Dutch East Indies. Some nights, as our bombers returned from their missions, the Japanese counted the number of planes missing in the formations and filled in with their own planes loaded with full tanks of fuel and bombs. Thinking that all of the returning planes showing on radar were our own, we did not send out the usual air raid warnings to the bases. Our area around Darwin was seldom hit, but Allied airfields along the track south to Alice Springs received some late-night surprises and casualties.

Between air raids and keeping a 24-hour watch on the Army network station in Darwin, I explored the city, its beaches, and interesting places. The station's one jeep was used for running messages to different locations, for stringing telephone wire to Allied camps, and to get out of the area in case the Japanese came ashore. But our motor pool mechanic, Sergeant Everhardt, found an abandoned motorcycle, and after some repairs on its front fender, we had two vehicles to get the eight of us out of the city.

Under a big, wide-open sky, I enjoyed my trips to the docks and to the RAAF airdrome, as well as the short trips to the Commanding Officers' quarters in a bombed-out building on Smith Street in the center of town. There were demolished buildings on either side of Cavanagh and Smith Streets, stretching from the governmental office buildings on a bluff above the harbor to Myilly Point and Larrakeyah Barracks, sticking out into the Timor Sea some three miles away.

One evening after sunset, two soldiers and I climbed into the jeep and went looking at the damage done during the first raid on Darwin. One block east of our Headquarters at the Toombul Flats, at a point overlooking the harbor, we examined several stone buildings that had been Darwin's administration buildings, police station, and other governmental offices before the raid. They were totally destroyed. Climbing between slivers of broken walls standing like ghosts in the moonlight, I looked down at the shimmering water in the harbor. It gave me an eerie feeling. The words of the song "On the road to Mandalay, where the flying fishes play" came to mind. Anger welled up in me. I was far from home, helplessly viewing the destruction of war. Before my arrival in Darwin, war was something I had read about but dismissed easily from my mind. Standing there in the rubble, as I looked at the devastation down Cavanagh and Smith Streets, I was overwhelmed with the realization that I had little defense against an enemy from the sky or from the beaches.

I had been issued thermite — high temperature — bombs to burn the radio station should the Japanese come ashore, but we had only the one jeep and motorcycle for the eight of us to get out of Darwin on the only road south. I knew I did not want to return down that miserable road across the thousands of miles of Australia's Outback.

American personnel in the Darwin city limits consisted of a First Sergeant, a cook, two motor pool mechanics, four radio operators, and our CO. Our Toombul Flats Headquarters was on the east end of the city, near the Hotel Darwin Ltd. on the bluff above the harbor. Neither the Flats nor the Hotel were hit by the Japanese bombers and fighter planes. The Americans' first Headquarters, on Smith Street near the center of town, had been almost completely demolished by a Japanese dive-bomber early in the war, though our Commanding Officer still used a room in the old headquarters for his office. I often delivered communiques to him there.

Our Signal Corps station was under a small garage, about 30 feet from the Flats, sand-bagged for protection. Trenches were dug in an open area to the west. Our war was a matter of waiting for Japanese raiders and hoping for no enemy invasion. Every day was eventful, with little time for thoughts of what might have been or what to do in case of danger. It was then that I began keeping a diary and writing of things going on around me.

At about that time, a war correspondent for a Chicago newspaper visited our area, and I was fascinated by the guy. A spark was ignited in me to put my impressions of the war and human reactions on paper for use later. I began scribbling notes on cards and slips of paper and stowing them in my A-bag. I began taking more pictures with my pocket-size Kodak Brownie camera, and an Aussie soldier in a dental lab developed my prints. None of them, however, got past U.S. censorship.

Our little station was kept busy with air raid warnings, network traffic, and sending damage reports and ship activities to Base Section One Headquarters at Adelaide River, some 50 miles south of Darwin. Using a 100-watt transmitter, a Hallicrafter receiver, and a 12-drop switchboard, we maintained 24-hour watch on the network — our primary mission. The rest of the time we worked at being soldiers and doing our duty.

Every day we scanned the skies for planes, and on the moonlit nights worried that Tojo would come calling. We did not face mortar attacks or trench warfare, but we were always conscious of the possibility of death from the skies. The thought of how many times I could be spared was always on my mind, and my anxiety began to build.

Some days, after we finished re-stringing telephone wire through the palm trees and bush to warehouses at Vestey's Meatworks and other installations, Vandy and I swam or walked Mindil and Fannie Bay beaches looking for seashells. Other days, Scotty, a QANTAS employee who owned a small crash boat with an outboard motor, took us around the harbor or back into the mangrove swamps where we stirred up crocodiles and birds. Scotty's main claim to fame was his availability in retrieving Allied pilots shot down in the immediate harbor or out in the Timor Sea. He and his boat were also our main supply line to freighters in the service of the Australian government, which generously issued all military personnel a weekly ration of cigarettes and liquor. Scotty was a popular guy.

Because of the isolation and smallness of our station, I became a cryptographer, encoding and decoding messages with an ingenious little instrument called an M-94 code-wheel. Developed by the U.S. Army Signal Corps back in the early 1920s, the device was a metal cylinder about eight inches long, holding 20 or so disks the size of silver dollars that could be spun on a central rod. Etched around the outer edge of each disk were the letters of the alphabet. After I set up the first two groups, or code key, these discs were spun around the rod and the letters in the message were lined up to make a sentence in English (ciphertext). Then the center rod was locked in place. Turning the cylinder over and holding it before me horizontally, I then selected any line on the opposite side of the text to construct a coded message for transmission. As was usual, the encoded letters were sent in groups of five and followed the first two key groups. These code key groups were what we gave to the Army signal stations around the world each morning.

Decoding or cryptanalyzing a coded message was the reverse of the encoding procedure, again using the same first two key groups. The message in English was then delivered to my CO. I quickly learned to use the little cylinder and guard it with my life. Larger Signal Corps centers had personnel schooled in these procedures and used machines for more rapid coding and ciphering of messages.

During nights when the network traffic was slow, I scanned the wavebands for stations broadcasting in code or voice to see who in the world was out there. I listened to Tokyo Rose and her babble on a powerful station from Tokyo. In her spiel she often mentioned "the 100,000 men in the Darwin area," reminding them how terribly lonesome they were while far from their wives and sweethearts and losing the war. But she played great American Big Band music.

Due to a phenomenon called skip effect, caused by radio waves bouncing off of the solar layers in the ionosphere, I picked up "The Grand Old Opry" from Tennessee on certain nights. At times, when there were high cirrus clouds or storms over the Pacific Ocean, I also tuned in the BBC, the British Broadcasting Company. It came in clear for five to ten minutes, depending on the angle that the radio waves bounced off the D, E, and F solar layers. I loved listening to the British accent during those short intervals. And a powerful station whose call letters were XERF, from Vicuna, Coahuila, Mexico, with programs in both English and Spanish, came in clear most of the time.

Our little station, designated as U.S. Advanced Headquarters, had just the three radio operators and myself to handle the large volume of traffic during a 24-hour period. Regulations required that we call Base Section One network Headquarters at Adelaide River every hour on the hour.

Because of the harassment by the Japanese bombers and lack of sleep, I was always asking for one more guy to help us at the station. When I learned that a wounded Filipino boy, who had escaped from Bataan's final days, was at a Darwin hospital, I went to visit him to see if he could be worked into our signal center.

Al Labasbas was a member of the Filipino Scouts, a highly respected group of soldiers specially trained in the Philippines. I provided him with a copy of the International Morse Code, and using the wooden floor under his hospital bed for a sounding board, he tapped out the dots and dashes until he could handle 10 to 12 words per minute, sufficient to send and receive the hourly call-ins on the network. Later, when he was dismissed from the Australian hospital, I worked him into our schedule with routine duties on the circuit.

From my journal:

August 9, 1943.

Written in Darwin, Northern Territory, Australia.

Al Labasbas — Philippino [*sic*] Scout

Arnulfo "Al" Labasbas is a member of the Philippino [*sic*] Scouts, a special trained group of soldiers who fought with General MacArthur's embattled troops in the Philippine Islands. I met him in the Darwin hospital where he was recovering from a broken leg incurred while escaping from Japanese soldiers on Bataan Peninsula in March 1942.

Before the war, Al lived near Manila in Sampaloc, Sorsogon, PI. He was the son of a farmer living in one of the provinces of the Philippine Islands. He had attended several agricultural schools and a banking school in Manila. He was attending the latter when the skies over Manila were first darkened by Japanese planes. While his outfit evacuated their position north of Bataan in the dead of the night the truck carrying him and his companions crashed into a tree. His companions were killed and he suffered a broken leg. He was without medical care for twelve hours and when brought to an American Field hospital in Bataan was given only a slight chance of survival by American nurses and doctors who cared for him. He was operated on without anesthesia for fear of his not regaining consciousness. . . .

After spending a short while in the underground hospital at Corrigedor he was put on the last hospital ship to leave the island bound for Australia. As the hospital ship pulled away from the beleaguered island he said he could hear the US coastal guns still shelling the Japanese. The hospital ship ran the Japanese blockade down past Mindinao and on to Darwin where he was hospitalized.

While he was with us Al was always restless and anxious to get back to the Philippines. He loved boats and the sea. One night while on duty he picked up a broadcast of an underground station from the Philippines. The broadcast was in Tagalog, the universal language of the islands, and he recognized the names of some in his outfit. They were still resisting the Japanese. From that time on he made plans to get back to his homeland.

Al did his job well and was a very disciplined soldier. One afternoon an Australian left a half of a 20-pound barracuda in our mess hall. Al cleaned it, seasoned it with spices found in our kitchen, then wrapped it in some banana leaves and buried it in a bed of coals in the ground. It was a real islanders' meal, and not our regular fare.

Then one morning Al was gone. Since he was not on any roster, he was free to leave. I hope he made it back to his people.

My first encounter with the aborigines had been the jackaroo with the floppy hat and flies at Birdum, down at U.S. Base Section One. My second encounter with these primitive men was more dramatic. One morning as I stepped around the corner of our quarters, I almost ran into three tall, nearly naked black men standing absolutely motionless, looking directly at me. One was holding a spear six-inches taller than he was. The spear had a flat, pointed metal tip and a long wooden shaft. Another fellow had some knives and forks we had left lying in the yard from a cookout three or four nights before. The third aborigine just stood there grinning. He was missing a tooth from a mouthful of perfect teeth. Later I learned the aborigine's tooth had been knocked out purposely during a ceremonial event in his clan to let mean spirits out.

These men had heavy eyebrows, high cheek bones, and broad noses. All aborigines that I saw had well-kept, soft wavy hair. They did not show aggressiveness, but carried themselves with an air of confidence. As these men stood motionless looking at me, I wondered where they originated, and who they were.

Webster's Dictionary defines the word aborigine as being "first" of a kind or a primitive inhabitant of a region. Anthropologists have differing versions of the exact origin of the Australian aborigines. But there were three of them standing in front of me, and they did not look as primitive or out of control as I did.

Over half of the population in the Darwin and surrounding bush were aborigines and half-castes. They were not ignorant people. With no formal education or modern tools, they survived in a harsh land. And I was the intruder, though not intentionally.

On another morning, one of the radio operators and I decided to explore the jungle outback of Darwin to see if we could see these aborigines in their natural setting. We took a jeep and started down a grassy sideroad leading off into thick bush. We were flushing out birds and lizards as we followed a narrow trail overgrown with tall grass and small trees. After about two miles, the scrub and trees got so dense that our jeep bumper couldn't clear the way anymore. We came to an opening and drove across a small stream where our jeep stopped against a tree. When we backed up to turn around, we felt someone was watching us. Standing motionless at the edge of the stream and holding a long spear at his side was a tall aborigine. About 20 feet from him was a female, crouched over a giant white clam shell. Something inside that shell moved — a baby kicking and rocking in a perfect shell cradle. We had intruded on the lives of a native family. I have not forgotten that violation, for no matter where you are in the world, your home and family are private. The aborigines watched silently as we drove back across the stream to make our way to town.

There was always something to do in the Darwin area. In my off-duty hours I also explored jungle trails or strolled the beaches fronted by the Indian Ocean, on the west side of Darwin. A displaced landlubber from the dry plains of Kansas, I was fascinated by the sea, its constant movement, and its soothing sounds.

Despite the discipline and regimentation inherent in being a member of the Armed Services, a soldier has lots of individual freedom during wartime. With room and board and finances provided for, one can often select and do as one chooses between duties, with proper preparation. Tempered by isolation on the farm when I was growing up, I liked being alone to sort out the whys and what-fors of my life. Strolling the beach had a therapeutic value for me, and I took advantage of the situation.

Darwin had one of the highest tides (28 feet) in the world. You could see fully 50 yards of beach with each tidal rise and fall; and it happened twice a day. Loading and unloading ships at the boom jetty and main wharf was always a challenge for dock workers in Darwin's inland harbor. Sometimes the ship was so low in the water the boom could not reach the cargo. But on Mindil and Fanny Bay beaches, about two miles from our dugout, on the Timor Sea, the tides left new and wide expanses of inviting sand for exploration.

One morning while checking the location of a trench under a line of palm trees just above the reach of the high tide, I found a prize, a seahorse shell, evacuated and in perfect shape. I stuck it in my suntan shirt pocket to join other small clam shells I had collected. When the morning sun grew hotter I took off my shirt and placed it on a wide sweep of sand so I could see it and not forget it on my way back down the beach. Upon returning, I picked up my shirt and naturally felt for the pretty shell. It was gone! I looked again where it had laid in the sand. Leading away from it were tiny tracks where something had dragged a shell. Following the tracks in the sand, I soon caught up with the culprit — a busy little hermit crab lugging his new home. How did it know to look in my shirt pocket? It must have been in the shell when I picked it up earlier. I had picked up its home. Forgetting all about the war, I became engrossed in getting a little creature to relinquish my shell. Well, it was really his shell.

Recalling the incident and the method that little crab used for its survival often afforded me solace and relaxation from the pressures of war later on. Survival often depended on one's initiative and attitude.

Another of my explorations had developed after we had been watching the outdoor cinema one night at Myilly Point. An Australian soldier had overheard our conversation, as we wondered where we would next venture. With his finest lingo he said, "I'll tell yer where to go, Yank. Tike the road out past the Wallaby dump. Keep gowin' 'til yer come to a narrow bit of a road. Turn left and follow it straight on. She'll run into a bloody big meadow. At sundown the 'roo are as thick as bloody flies miking their way to 'igher ground. It's a bonzer spot for the natives and local blokes," he reckoned.

"Yer won't believe it, Yank, 'til yer see it," he continued. Then looking us straight in the eye he added, "Dinkie di!" (On the level!)

Making sure everything was in order at the station, Vandy and I left one afternoon for the road back into the area described by the Aussie. A couple of miles into the bush, we happened upon a kangaroo laying among some sharp rocks about 30 yards off the road on a small ridge. We were about to drive on by when I hollered to Vandy to stop. Something in the brush had moved.

We stopped and climbed up to the top of the ridge. We found the kangaroo was dead, but there was a baby in the mother's pouch. Two big ears and a pointed nose were sticking out as we turned over the mother to extract the little Joey.

"Let's take it back to the station," I said excitedly.

We wrapped the squirming little 'roo in my shirt and walked back down the hill.

Our Aussie friend at the cinema had described an expansive lowland full of tall grass through which kangaroos had made numerous paths. Every evening hundreds of kangaroos in one big body moved out of the edge of the surrounding bush and migrated en masse across the meadow to the shadows under the tall timber on the far side. I imagined it being similar to the movement of buffalo across the plains of Kansas in the 1800s.

We drove on toward the big meadow and arrived there just before sundown. We parked on a promontory overlooking an expansive sea of dry kunai grass stretching in front of us for more than a half-mile. Sure enough, hundreds of kangaroos moved slowly across the wide meadow.

Like an army deployed in a firefight, an ocean of bobbing kangaroos, some six feet tall, popped their heads above the grass as they moved past us. They followed a pattern of hopping, grazing, and standing erect with just their heads above the vegetation. A thumping sound of feet on grassy paths drummed across the landscape.

We were overcome with awe as we watched the undulating horde progress into the darkening shadows behind us. As the sun disappeared into the timber, we left that sea of bobbing heads, turned the jeep around, and headed back to the station. We had almost forgotten our little friend kicking around in my shirt on the back seat of the jeep.

We arrived back at the station before dark and immediately inspected our prize. When sitting on its tail, the baby kangaroo was the size of a jackrabbit. We decided to keep it in the radio room so that it couldn't escape. We couldn't tell its sex, so we called it "Connie" for either Constance or Conrad. When it started chewing on its tail, it dawned on us that it was hungry, and so we found a small can of condensed milk in the mess hall and mixed one part milk to four parts water. One of the men had an eye dropper, which we could use for feeding, and we were in the nursery business.

There is some kind of an instinct in humans that makes them want to cuddle and nurse the helpless. Everybody wanted to hold and feed Connie. In a matter of hours, that kangaroo was all over the room, even hopping around on top of the hot transmitter.

Because a baby kangaroo spends nearly all of its time in its mother's pouch, we looked around for something comparable, so that it would feel at home with us. One of the guys found a thick, knitted Red Cross sock that his mother had sent to him in the hot jungles — for fear he would catch cold! We hung the sock "à la Claus" on an electric cord stretched across the top of our transmitter on a table about three feet off of the floor. When we held the little Joey up to the entrance of the sock, it dived in head first and did a complete U-turn, ending up with its mouth and tail sticking out of the sock together. It grabbed the end of its tail and started sucking.

The heat from the transmitter kept the little 'roo warm during the cool nights. We had a neat makeshift nursery for our babe of the woods. It worked perfectly, and we took turns feeding or taking our prized exhibit on walkabouts for its relief.

We established a schedule and all was going well until around 10

Al Labasbas, a Filipino Scout, at the entrance to our underground radio station in Darwin in the summer of 1943. *Ray Wyatt photo*

o'clock one morning while Al Labasbas was on duty. I was dead asleep when Al came yelling, "Smoke! Smoke! Kangaroo in smoke!"

By the time I reached the entrance of the underground door I could see the the blackened cloud curling out of the room. It was billowing up from the center of the transmitter where a sock-full of kangaroo was bouncing and gyrating uncontrollably in the middle of it all. I quickly disconnected the transmitter and untied the electric cord holding Connie. Someone pulled the 'roo out of the sock and took it outside and turned it loose. It hopped around free at last, and started chasing a dog roaming

Spearing fish off the northwest coast is an international event near Darwin. Three aborigines demonstrate how it's done to an American soldier, an Australian sailor and an Australian soldier (sitting).
Commonwealth of Australia, Department of Information

One Australian soldier watches for crocodiles while the others swim in a river near Katherine, in the Northern Territory.
Commonwealth of Australia, Department of Information

Ant castles in the Northern Territory of Australia. *Ray Wyatt photo*

On pay day, in the Australian Territory, "diggers" played "2-up," a game similar to an American crap game. Americans used one coin and bet on it landing heads or tails up. Australians tossed up two coins with a paddle and bet on their landing two up, the same sides, either heads or tails. There are three rings of players here.

the neighborhood. Connie was okay, but our radio room had a pungent smell of urine in it. Connie had peed in the sock, causing urine to run down into the transmitter, shorting out two tubes.

Alas! Our transmitter was shot, our nursery destroyed, and we were off the air. After many tries we contacted Base Section One Headquarters at Adelaide River and requested a transmitter repairman. We were back on the air in a couple of days, and luckily the Japanese had not sent any planes over in the interim. The transmitter repairman made up an explanation to Headquarters about our being off the air, and we escaped a reprimand for our adventure in kangaroo raising.

From that experience we learned that Connie, the kangaroo, preferred the freedom of the Outback to the Yankee dugout. When it was released, it lost its cute baby ways. It became just another inhabitant of the animal world trying to survive on its own.

My first fishing trip in the tropics was another of my "wildlife" explorations in Darwin. From my journal:

FISHING IN DARWIN

April 20, '43

At 4 o'clock in the afternoon Corporal Tilton, another radio operator, and a character named Pokoi from Chicago, woke me and asked if I wanted to go fishing. I said, "Yeah, sure. Where do we go?"

"Down at the docks," they replied. "It's a bonzer place. Lots of Aussies there, too."

We grabbed some fishing lines and a small net for use in catching bait and took off. . . . "Down at the docks" was the pier where the Japs had sunk the British merchant ship Neptuna some months before. The old ship lay on its side in about 20 feet of water with a portion of its hull wedged against the docks out of the water. An Australian soldier told us there were still 12 bodies in her hold.

While we were quietly dipping our net under one side of the pier for "Greenies," large minnows, an Aussie soldier came along and said, "Hey Yank! Try the other side. There's a good lot of them there. Give 'er a fair go, Yank!"

With only a few dips of the net we easily got enough bait for the evening's try. Tilton pointed toward the end of the pier about 100 yards out and said, "Look at the crowd out there, Pokoi. I told you we should have been down here a half hour ago."

We walked out to the end of the pier where several Australians were trying their luck. They didn't seem to be catching anything. We each cast our lines made of quarter-inch clothes line with a No. 9 nail bent into a hook on which we placed our "Greenie" bait. Tilton was the first to catch one. . . . It was about 18 inches long and weighed about 5 pounds. . . . Then something hit my line. I tugged on my rope. It was a shade smaller than Tilton's, but who cared? The biggest fish I had ever caught back in Kansas was a 10 inch catfish. I asked an Aussie standing behind me, "Hey Cobber, what are these?"

"They're mackerel," he said.

. . . The secret to our success was the "Greenie" bait we were using. The Aussies were using meat and insects for their bait.

As Tilton hooked one about 22 inches long and weighing about 10 pounds, some Aussie behind us said, "Gawd stone the blinkin' crows. Would yer look at that?" In a few minutes we three Yanks were standing shoulder to shoulder plying our lines. . . . Free as the breeze, we American GIs were catching big fish in a foreign country far from home. All three of the fish were about the same size . . . each about 17 pounds and over 2 feet long.

The crowd just stood there watching.

We had caught about 17 . . . all mackerel.

They took several of the smaller ones and we picked up the remainder . . . , 7 big ones, and started back across the pier to the jeep.

Walking along on the planks placed across the bombed out portion of the pier we could see Australian naval vessels and a few small fishing boats in the harbor. The sun had just gone down and the water across the way was like a beautiful blue mirror. Swinging along carrying our fish it felt great to be alive. The lights from several small boats reflected on the still water and voices came clear and distinct across the way. From the deck of one of the ships some Australian sailors recognized Pokoi in the gloom and shouted, "Hey Yank! 'ow about one of your big ones for our evening scran, eh?"

Pokoi said, "Sure thing, Cobbers . . . for your beer issue this week."

"Awh. Give us a fair go, Yank."

We kept going. On the way to our quarters Pokoi said, "Let's give a couple to the Aussie nurses down at the hospital. I promised them one, and a couple to the Red Shield [Red Cross] too. We can only eat two of them."

We were home in about 5 minutes and grabbed a snack out of the rations stored in our headquarters. The moon was up and full. The night was as bright as day. . . .

At midnight I was back on duty in the radio room waiting for the Japanese to do their thing. My first fishing trip in the tropics was a fascinating event.

Early the next morning I received a phone call requesting someone to

British Mark VC Spitfires under camouflage at the Royal Australian Air Force Airdrome in Darwin, Northern Territory, in March 1943. *Ray Wyatt photo*

Photo of an American Spitfire pilot from the American Eagle Squadron formerly located in England. *Ray Wyatt photo*

Vandy Vanderpool and the author were stringing Signal Corps wires in palm trees to Vestey's Warehouse just before a big Japanese air raid in Darwin, in June 1943. Vanderpool is in the tree. *Ray Wyatt photo*

A sign on Mindil Beach in Darwin points toward Japan some 5,000 miles away, in April 1943. *Ray Wyatt photo*

The PBY Catalina Flying Boat Ray Wyatt was in as a side gunner on a mission in Darwin, Northern Territory, in May 1943. *Ray Wyatt photo*

A Japanese "Zero" fighter plane crash near Darwin, May 1943. *Ray Wyatt photo*

assist a physician of the Royal Flying Doctor Service who was taking a white man to Leper Island, an isolated spot about a mile east across the big harbor, and inaccessible from the land side. I agreed to go. One of the guys took me to the docks where I met the doctor waiting in a small motor boat with his patient.

The patient was a stocky-built white Australian, perhaps in his mid-forties. He was aware of what had happened to him. He believed he had gotten leprosy at a bore (well) near an aborigine settlement north of Alice Springs on the north-south track.

Most of the inhabitants of Leper Island were natives of the Northern Territory. The doctor said this patient was the first white man to be taken there, from which there was no return.

After a half-hour's ride across the harbor, we docked at a rocky beach. I asked the doctor if I could go ashore, and he agreed, but set limits as to how far I could venture. The main part of the Leper settlement was behind the brow of a hill. The doctor and his patient went on ahead and I stayed near the boat.

There was little vegetation around the dock area, but I could see small

Some of Australia's finest. The "diggers" were a "bonzer mob" and eager to get stuck into the action.
Commonwealth of Australia, Department of Information

Australian servicemen didn't let a war stop their love of horse racing. This is the Darwin Cup Day in the Northern Territory, 1943.

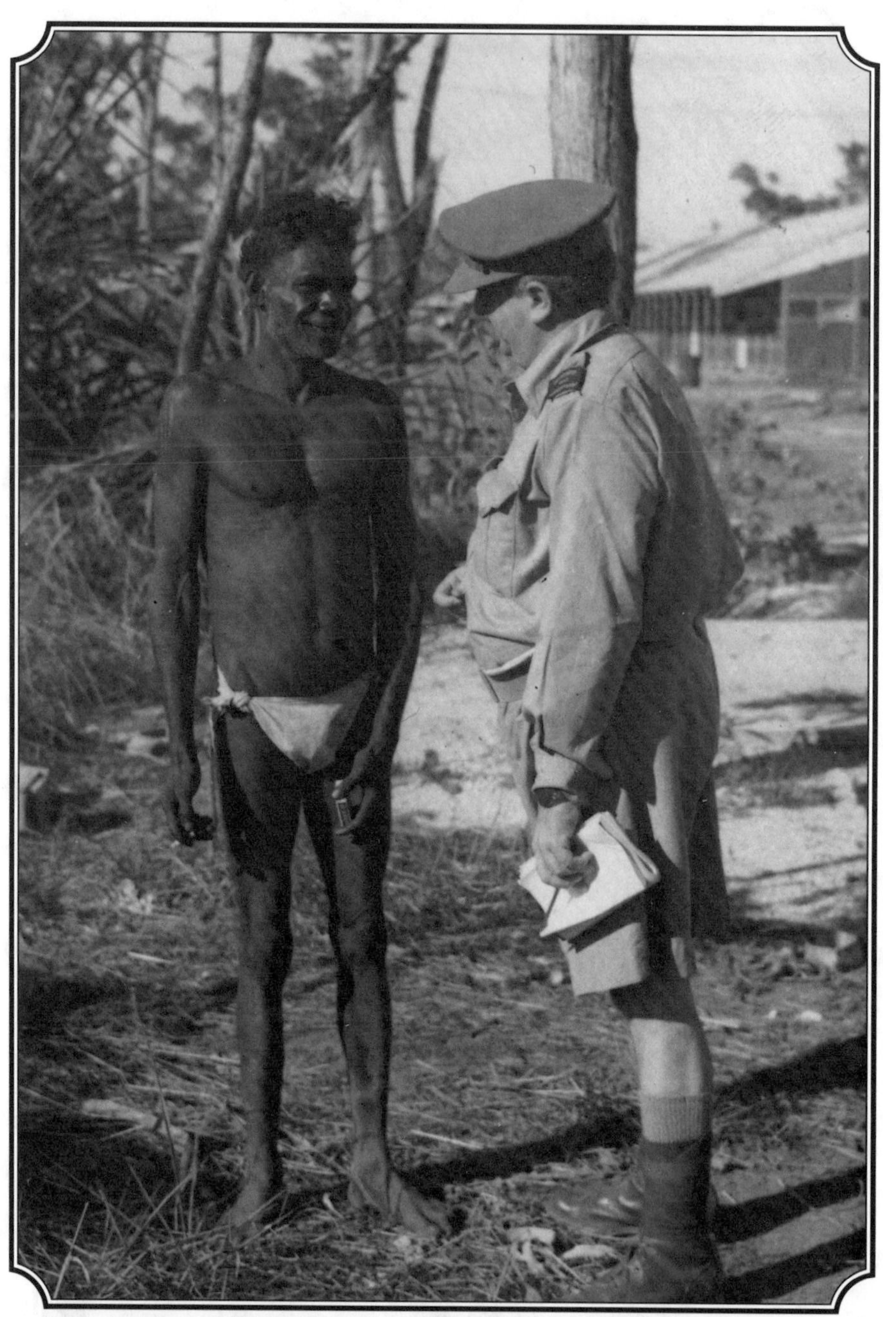

Most aborigines were friendly people, as shown here talking to an Australian officer in Darwin. Note the package of cigarettes in the aborigine's left hand.
Commonwealth of Australia, Department of Information

Aborigines in front of their bark homes in the Top End — Northern Territory — of Australia.
Commonwealth of Australia, Department of Information

Aborigine men reenact events of the day in a ceremony called a "corrobboree." *Commonwealth of Australia, Department of Information*

Most aborigine men were over six feet tall, with whiskers. They were hardy, well-built people.
Commonwealth of Australia, Department of Information

shrubs and grass farther inland. The doctor was met by two Catholic nuns in gleaming white garb, from an order known as the Sisters of Charity. They soon disappeared over the crest of the hill.

Wanting something to do, I walked toward a group of small wooden structures similar to our outhouse back on the farm. There was somebody in nearly every one of them, and I kept my distance. The women wore clean light dresses and the men had a loin cloth tied in a knot around their waist. Looking closer, I saw that parts of their sun-calloused bodies were eaten away by leprosy. When they looked at me, I had to look away. It was an involuntary reaction, and it embarrassed me. I turned back toward the beach for the shelter of the boat.

The doctor soon came back over the hill alone. As he walked down to the boat landing I saw a fellow with a leg dangling by a tendon hobbling toward us. He gave us a big smile and waved. I hadn't the courage to wave back and quickly got into the boat. But I thought of the verse in the Bible, "When Jesus saw one leper who had returned He said, 'Were not 10 made clean?'"

It was not because of the number on the island, but because of the isolation and agony of that crippling disease that I vowed never to take my health and my life for granted again. I could not imagine the courage it took to live on that island. Dodging Japanese bombs didn't seem too bad right then.

As I rode back to Darwin, my thoughts turned to introspective awareness of what had sustained me until the present day. My spirituality had been given support by our military establishment. Church service for United States servicemen was made available during the war whether on board ship or under a canopy of trees in the jungle. To the credit of our military, chaplains and religious leaders were important in the lives of displaced men and women.

I attended church whenever possible while stationed in Melbourne. But when I had entered the Australian Outback at Mount Isa, in upper Queensland, they told me the only church available was at Darwin, nearly 1,000 miles away. When we got to Base One Section Headquarters at Adelaide River in the Northern Territory, I inquired about religious services. I was told that a Catholic chaplain would hold services at an Australian stockman's shack on the next Sunday morning.

On the appointed day, I went to the designated place where a dozen men, both American and Australian, were gathered in a truly primitive setting. The service was in a stable with two horse stalls inside a lean-to hut about a mile from camp. A Catholic priest stood behind a small table with his back to the manger and his paraphernalia for saying Mass laid out before him. The location reminded me of Joseph and Mary 2,000 years ago in Bethlehem when Christ was born. The priest informed us that we had been granted special dispensation from fasting or going to Confessions before receiving Communion while we were in combat zones. That eased my conscience! The rest of the day seemed easier after a church service.

Darwin's little church was about six blocks west of our quarters. It was not as inspiring as the rustic stable back near Adelaide River, but it was a visual reminder for us of the ravages of war. Two life-sized angels looked down from each side of the altar, adding an appropriate setting for Mass. Somewhat disruptive to my thoughts were bullet holes in pews and artifacts. The most evident were three chunks missing from the wing of one of the angels on the right side altar. The Japanese fighter pilots would have been amazed to learn they had hit angels as they strafed streets and buildings in Darwin! But it didn't deter our Allied soldiers from their religious pursuits. Our chaplains were appreciated and regarded with highest respect by everyone involved during World War II. They were the quiet heroes.

One afternoon, with no previous communications I got a call from some Seabees who had gotten off of a ship in Port Darwin. On shore they were billeted in an old barracks or warehouse a few blocks from our location.

The Seabees, the Construction Battalions of the U.S. Navy, was established in December 1941 to build landing facilities and airfields in combat areas and rebuild or build installations wherever needed. I'm not sure why they were in Darwin. Perhaps they were on their way to the Philippines or Dutch New Guinea.

I went to their quarters and explained that the Japanese might bomb the place that night, since there would be a full moon. I said that I would call them, and gave them the "Yellow" and "Red" bomb alert signals.

The Seabees crowded around and asked more questions about where the pubs were, were there any women, and/or good restaurants in town. They must have just come from the States.

Sure enough, that night the Japanese sent over a group of bombers and scattered their eggs around the harbor. I stayed in the dugout and sent the usual ZZZ Air-raid "Yellow" to all my list, including the Seabees. In less than two minutes an Aussie switch called.

"Some of yer blokes are running up and down the road 'ere, Mite. My bloody oath. One of them 'as nothing on but 'is 'elmet. Another just went by like a flaming emu dragging 'is strides (pants). They are running past each other in different directions. Who are these blokes?"

It took me a second or two to visualize the action he described. Then I knew it was our Seabees. I had neglected to tell them where to take cover. But then there were no trenches for them anyway.

The Japanese raids over Darwin continued to disrupt our adventures and made us aware there was a war to be won.

A phenomenon that surfaced during World War II was the sudden insatiable appetite of servicemen and defense workers for reading material — surely a surprise to anthropologists and many high school English teachers in America.

All Americans like to read. Hidden or stifled for years, this sudden urge to hold, thumb, and read anything came full force when servicemen found themselves unoccupied for a few moments. Most cherished were letters from home, followed closely by the hometown newspaper. Members of the Armed Forces wanted to know such tidbits as who had dodged the Draft, who had gotten married, or pregnant, or joined up. Most disruptive in their lives were the Dear John letters: "Dear John: I couldn't wait. I married Joe Doe from down the street. I know you can find someone else. Please understand."

Some sent home photos in hopes they could get their picture in the paper for their gallantry in the mess hall.

By far the most abundant and sought-after reading matter were the small paperbacks, touching everything from romance to mysteries to athletics. Another most sought-for publication was the company newsletter, an in-house organ telling of your outfit's accomplishments or replacements. I was a "stringer" (reporter) for the *Cockatoo*, a publication put out by the 997th Signal Service Company in Australia's Northern Territory. Other publications in the South Pacific were the *New Guinea Gold*,

Jungle Rot, *YANK*, *Stars and Stripes*, and my favorite, the *Southern Cross Bulletin*, published in Finschhafen. Now and then we could get a copy of the major newspaper booklets such as *Bluey and Curly* by Melbourne's *Sun Herald*.

Every piece of reading material got super reader coverage. Dog-eared and raggedy books of all kinds could be found any time under the gunwales of ships, in latrines (poopdeck), and in every barracks and camp around the world. Like Kilroy, they could be found in the most unlikely places.

The favorite newsman of all combat troops was Ernie Pyle, who followed men into action to do his reporting. His dedication to his fighting men led to his death by a sniper's bullet on Ie Shima Island near the Island of Japan on June 10, 1945.

My hat is off to all the great reporters and photographers who risked their lives in order to keep everyone informed on the homefront and those overseas. Like our chaplains, they did not ask to be heroes.

Japanese raids over Darwin continued to disrupt our explorations and adventures, and made us aware there was a war to be won. The last raid on the city was in late November 1943. Since there were no more targets left in the immediate area, the Japanese bombed Allied airbases south along the track, and on south to other airfields, particularly Mataranka and Fenton airfields, south of Darwin. The need for fighters to defend the Darwin area had diminished. The war had moved on.

The need for the ZZZ air-raid warning had become unnecessary, and I felt that I should move too, if Army regulations would permit. Surely the jungles of New Guinea were more intriguing than this. I applied for R&R, and to my surprise, the request was granted. I was soon to find out about conditions in the New Guinea area where the war was raging full blast.

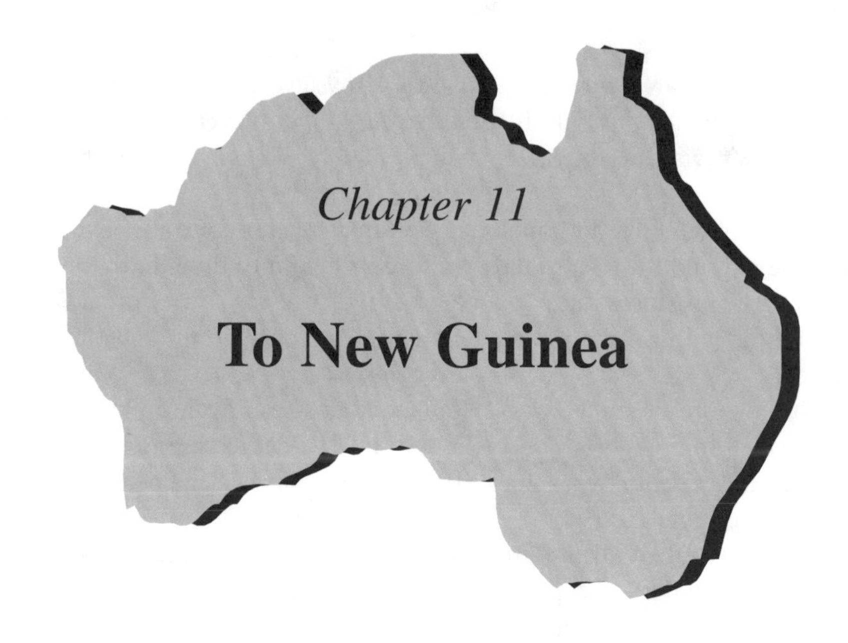

Chapter 11

To New Guinea

LATE IN NOVEMBER 1943, my R&R was approved, and afterwards, I was to report in to Base Section Four Melbourne, in two weeks, for a new assignment. I was glad to leave Darwin because the air raids had subsided and Army life had become too routine. If the Japanese had my name on one of their bombs, they had waited too long to deliver it. I had been lucky so far.

One of the Signal Corps guys took me to Fenton Field, where I carried my A- and B-bags onto a C-47 Gooney Bird going south to Adelaide. The pilot was a young dogface who hadn't passed navigator school, but he told me not to worry. After we were airborne and on a steady course, I asked him, just to be friendly, if we were flying on the "beam." He said, "Hell, no! There are no beams in Australia. I just point this thing south and pull back on the stick." Then as an afterthought he muttered, "I hope to hell I never have to ditch this thing in this God-forsaken country."

I told him that back in the States before I enlisted and war broke out I wanted to work for TWA as a radio operator. Commercial pilots in the late 1930s had to fly a designated route and follow a steady radio signal called a beam that kept them on course from city to city. If weather or other conditions caused a pilot to drift off of the steady radio beam, he would be alerted by a beeping *dot-dash* (**A**) in the left quadrant, or a *dash-dot* (**N**) in the right quadrant. When a pilot heard either of these signals, he simply pulled his plane back on the beam, a steady tone where they overlapped.

I told my pilot now over the vast Australian desert that it was important to stay on the beam. But he didn't get it and said he didn't need a beam to get to Alice Springs and a cold beer. He had a point. There was nothing to see on the ground from horizon to horizon. No cities. No tall buildings. No smoke. No livestock. Nothing. Just red dirt. I wondered what I would do if he had to set the plane down in that desolate, sweltering desert terrain.

As we cruised along in the big open sky over the bleak land below, the plane's motors hummed a monotonous tune and I relaxed. I looked around at some of the cargo and noticed a lot of boxes and miscellaneous equipment. There standing upright in the center of the load was a Wurlitzer nickelodeon! It kept shifting back and forth each time the plane hit a little airpocket. It looked just like the machine in Abe's Cafe back home where we high school kids used to listen to Glenn Miller's "In The Mood" and "String of Pearls." I could imagine what it would look like now if lit up.

I hollered to the pilot above the roar of the plane, "That's a nickelodeon back there isn't it?"

He yelled back, "Sure as hell is."

"Where did it come from? How did you get it,?" I hollered.

He yelled back, "Came from Milne Bay Officers Club. There must be a hundred of them down there in the mud and muck of New Guinea since the Americans left."

I hollered "Oh?" Then as I thought about it I quietly said, "Oh!"

Alice Springs, on the very bottom of the Northern Territory, from the air didn't look to be much except hard-packed earth with a few narrow streets bordered by spinifex grass and bush. The pilot said there were about 1,000 people there, a lot of them half-castes. No one was particularly interested in counting — just minding their own business. At the halfway point on the north-south track — the only one in central Australia

— 1,100 miles south of Darwin, and nearly 1,100 miles north of Adelaide, South Australia, on a mostly dirt and rutted road, Alice Springs was an important link in this part of the country. It had become famous during the first part of this century as the center for Dr. Flynn's Flying Doctor Service and the Radio School of the Air for the children of stockmen families in the far-out Outback. Now it was the main supply route to Allied camps in the Northern Territory of Australia.

It is estimated that over 200,000 Allied soldiers (Australian, Dutch, American, British, and Canadian) traversed the Northern Territory during the course of the war.

After taxiing up to some sunbaked buildings with corrugated iron roofing, the pilot quickly parked the plane and took off for town about a half-mile away. An Australian soldier on leave, waiting like me to catch a ride going south, told me the town got its name from an artesian well that sprang from a wash providing the only water available in this desert country. A governmental administrator "named it Alice Springs after his wife," he said.

"She must have been thrilled," I replied. You're a nobody until you have been to the "Alice."

Out near the airstrip west of town I found a stable where I bedded down for the night on a mattress of grass and stalks. Gazing around, I saw a half-caste female moving about in the bush as if she were cooking a meal. That was life in a most primitive form.

The grass mattress there in the stable didn't seem too bad. I ate some K-rations, slept soundly all night, and awoke refreshed the next morning. It was late fall in Australia, and the weather was beginning to get hot in the daytime. It wasn't bad. I was beginning to enjoy my first day of leave. At least there weren't any Japanese air raids to worry about!

Leaving Alice Springs the next morning, we flew along the east side of a glowing red monolith visible off to the southwest. The pilot said it was called Ayers Rock and was of religious significance to the aboriginal people. It was an awesome sight in the early morning sunlight. We could see Ayers Rock from the plane for a full five minutes as we flew on south toward Adelaide.

After a few hours we landed in Adelaide, a beautiful city on the southern Australian coast along the Indian Ocean. The city was landscaped with trees and grassy parks interspersed among its buildings, all intact— a real contrast to bombed-out Darwin. Adelaide was called the city of beautiful churches. I was impressed with its cleanliness and its beaches of white sand. A taxi driver informed me that many of Adelaide's settlers came from Ireland and Scotland as well as England. That, he said, accounted for the numerous blond and red-haired people in this lovely city by the sea.

Allied Services had selected a five-storied hotel for servicemen on R&R. The taxi took me directly to it. The hotel lobby had a large dining room, which I could see was full of military men. After checking in, I joined some of my countrymen and their Australian girlfriends at one of the big tables in the diner. I was about to order a meal when a nicely dressed blond took a seat beside me. Her sister and her catch for the evening sat across from us.

We introduced ourselves and I began to enjoy a conversation with a real live young woman. Later on, we joined three other couples and went to a movie in downtown Adelaide. Thus began three days and nights of socializing by walking, talking, and dining with young ladies, the first I had seen in dresses since December 1942 — a year earlier.

The morning before I was to leave Adelaide for Melbourne, where I had planned to spend most of my R&R, I found myself purposely left alone with my young Australian ladyfriend, Joan, in her sister's apartment. Much to my surprise, she made a move to seduce me, but my parent's lingering instructions to "always do the right thing" proved to be the insulation I needed to thwart her amorous advances. I retreated rather hastily to the hotel to pack for Melbourne. Joan agreed to see me off at the train station that afternoon, however.

As we sat on a grassy slope overlooking the railway station there in Adelaide, Joan began crying. She sobbed out a story of how she had become pregnant by another American soldier and had tried to get me to make love to her so that I could be blamed for her condition and be forced to marry her. She said she and her sister were daughters of a "cocky" (small) farmer not far from Adelaide, and had moved into the big city for work. She didn't have any money and was sorry for what she had tried to do to me. Gad! What could I do? I forgave her, of course, and really felt sorry for her. I pulled out 60 quid and handed it to her. As she walked with me down to the station, I regretted leaving the peaceful atmosphere of Adelaide. But life goes on and I had a new destination.

Shortly after the train left, we came to the Murray River crossing. Looking out the window, I saw an unbelievable herd of jackrabbits or hares so thick one couldn't count them all. They moved across the landscape in waves. I had heard of Australia's "rabbit fence" running north and south, but I wasn't sure which side of the river we were on. Some rabbits were in burrows along the banks of the Murray and some were moving out across the hillside. I tried counting them, using a method I had learned in forecasting potential insect damage to crops on the farm. I judged there to be one rabbit in every square yard. Looking up the hillsides and along the Murray River's bottomland I could see countless rabbits to the acre. I could see that Australia had a problem. The rest of the 10-hour trip was made under cover of darkness and was uneventful.

After alighting from the train in the Melbourne station the next morning, I walked past several coaches full of wounded soldiers from the battles in the Solomon Islands and New Guinea. I received the surprise of my life! There on a stretcher with a big toothy smile was Bradley, the guy who had told the lurid stories of his sexual escapades in Hollywood as we sailed aboard ship 18 months earlier. He had been wounded in Guadalcanal. I was glad to see him. He told me he had taken nine bullets in various parts of his body. I asked if he remembered the *Tasker H. Bliss* and the trip coming over? He did, and remembered as well my singing on the hot deck each evening. We reminisced briefly on where we had been and what had happened in the war so far. Some of the ambulatory patients with him were new recruits who had shot themselves in the foot after being thrown into the action on Guadalcanal, but at least they were alive.

After a good visit the medics took him away. When we parted this time I felt differently about him. His life was as valuable as the next guy, and I realized that I had no right to have judged him earlier.

In Melbourne, I stayed at an Allied Servicemen Comfort Station on North Collins Street. While there I got a letter from Joan. She needed more money. She threatened to accuse me of her pregnancy with her sister as a witness. I answered that letter promptly and wrote her a sermon on being a decent, responsible person. I didn't hear from her again.

Once again I enjoyed Melbourne and walking down Swanston Street and sitting on the grass in St. Kilda Park. One morning I took a bus tour of Healesville Sanctuary, outside Melbourne's city limits. There in that lush wooded area I saw a platypus swimming under a rocky ledge of a shallow stream. Near the top of some tall eucalyptus trees, several furry gray koala bears munched on eucalyptus leaves. But the constant cawing of magpies and other birds in that otherwise beautiful sanctuary surrounded by fern trees annoyed me as we walked through the park. After all, I was on R&R for peace and quiet.

At one point, the tour guide told me he had saved my life. According to him I was about to kick a kangaroo lying asleep in our path. An angered kangaroo or a wallaby could rip a person or another kangaroo or dog to pieces with its sharp pointed toes. I was more cautious after that.

In the days that followed I went to Luna Park, walked St. Kilda Road, visited the ANZAC (Australia and New Zealand Army Corps) Memorial, bet on the horses at Flemington Racecourse, sat on the banks of the Yarra River, bought apples from a Greek fruit stand, and ate lunch in cafes on Swanston Street. It was not a time filled with excitement and debauchery, but a natural way to savor the ambiance and laid-back lifestyle of Melbourne and Australia, our dependable ally.

With nearly a week left on my R&R, I went on a double date with a GI named Smith. He was from a wealthy family in St. Louis, a suave, good-looking, fast-talker. As a farm boy, I considered him a lady's man. Our evening with the young ladies was great, and a good time was had by all, but for some unknown reason, the next day I received special orders sending me to Finschhafen, New Guinea, a combat zone! I later learned that Smith had dated the Captain's girlfriend and I was guilty by association. The Captain said they needed radio operators in New Guinea. That's life; but it shortened my R&R.

Alone again and with travel orders in my hand, I bought a ticket on a small commercial plane to Sydney. My orders did not state a time to report in at Finschhafen. They simply read to report to Company Headquarters upon arrival. With a whole day to kill, I decided to see the sights of Sydney. Quite by accident I happened onto a captured Japanese midget submarine being exhibited near its beached location in Sydney Harbor. This Japanese cylindrical piece of equipment was about 30 feet long, with a tiny conning tower and periscope. Two Japanese had manned the sub by lying on their stomachs the entire time it was operable. The torpedoes carried in its hull could be released by both of its crew members. It was said that there had been two of these midget subs sunk in Sydney Harbor. This one had slipped the harbor defensive net only to be spotted by the Royal Australian Navy and blown out of the water.

The midget submarine was a Japanese ploy to create panic in Australia. And so, when nobody was looking, I walked over and gave it a good kick in the side.

Before leaving Sydney I rested on a grassy slope beside a large square building in downtown Hyde Park. To my surprise, several important-looking men emerged from the building wearing robes and curly white wigs — shades of merry old England! I couldn't imagine our Congressmen dressed in that fashion.

Later I strolled into Sydney's Allied Servicemen's club full of American GIs and Australian "diggers." While I was there, two sunburned blokes dressed in shorts and wearing big floppy hats offered to sell me some uncut opal stones. Not knowing what I was looking at, I turned them down. I could have bought the whole poke for a song! Dumb American GI!

Following a good rest, I caught a flight out of Sydney for Townsville for the trip across the Coral Sea to Port Moresby, Papua New Guinea. At Townsville, after an hour's layover, I caught a ride with the pilot of an A-20 Havoc twin-engine attack plane going north to Port Moresby. What a ride! That daredevil flew at about 100 feet above the blue water in what was the fastest trip I had ever taken — anywhere! As we zoomed over the water, I could see coral reefs below and once thought we were going to join them. Had he dunked the plane, there would have been no time for even a Hail Mary!

We landed at Ward's Field in Port Moresby in the evening. I stayed in an Army camp on the west side of town. The next morning I loaded both A- and B-bags onto a C-47 already overloaded with 17 GIs and their gear. We took off for Finschhafen, flying a route through a gap in the Owen Stanley Mountains where some peaks reach 13,000 feet. As we barely cleared the top, I looked down at the wreckages of other C-47s that hadn't made it. That was a rather discomforting sight.

After we landed on a newly constructed steel-mesh PSP — Pierced Steel Planking — runway at Finschhafen, the ground crew pointed to a plane losing altitude over the jungle. The pilot had radioed to the tower that he was out of gas. I learned later that no one survived the crash of that C-47. Welcome to New Guinea.

Chapter 12

Finschhafen, New Guinea

NEW GUINEA, just to the north of Australia, is the second largest island in the world, with mountain peaks over 13,000 feet high running southeast to northwest up and down its territory. Shaped like a bloated, warty, crocodile it is 1,500 miles long and 500 miles wide at the center.

Not all of the northern coast of New Guinea was ideal for amphibious landings; the center presented a real hazard for aircraft flying over the Owen Stanley Mountains.

Official languages in New Guinea at one time were English, Motu, and Pidgin (English). Over 700 local languages were spoken throughout the island.

Papua New Guinea was named by a Portuguese navigator using a Malay word meaning "woolly-haired." And during the New Guinea Campaign of World War II, Australians called these natives the "Fuzzy-Wuzzies" because of their gigantic hair style. These Melanesian island people are often confused with the taller Australian aborigines who had softer, wavy hair. However, the Papuans were village people whereas the aborigines were nomadic. The west half of New Guinea was Dutch Netherlands and Indonesian.

Finschhafen was a hot, swampy Papuan village along the north coast of the island of New Guinea, on the tip of the Huon Peninsula across from the island of New Britain in the Bismarck Archipelago. Just six degrees below the equator, it was a supply base for Japanese strikes at Lae, Salaumaua, Buna-Gona, the Kokoda Trail, Morobe, and Dobodura along the north coast, where some of the fiercest fighting took place during the New Guinea Campaign. To the east was Guadalcanal in the Solomon Islands; to the north was New Britain Island in the Bismarck Archipelago, and New Ireland, and Bougainville, all part of Australian Mandated Territory. Farther southeast, toward New Zealand, were the New Hebrides and New Caledonia Islands where the 37th and Americal Divisions were staged early in the SWPA action. (The Americal was the only U.S. division formed outside the continental United States.)

Before the war, Rabaul, on New Britain Island, was the capital of the Australian Mandated Territory. On January 22, 1942, six weeks after the attack on Pearl Harbor, the Japanese occupied Rabaul with some 100,000 troops. With an excellent harbor and available air strips, it became their headquarters for the intended invasion of Australia.

Following the fall of Rabaul to the Japanese, Lae, a seaport in the Huon Gulf south of Finschhafen, became the capital of Papua New Guinea. Then Lae fell to the Japanese in May. Port Moresby, on the south coast facing Australia and the Coral Sea, became Allied Headquarters and the major supply base for the New Guinea Campaign.

One of the decisive naval battles of the New Guinea Campaign was fought on March 3, 1943, in what is known as the Battle of the Bismarck Sea. In a major effort to reinforce embattled troops at Buna, Lae, and Salamaua, the Japanese sent eight destroyers and eight transports carrying 7,000 troops of the 51st Division into the Bismarck Sea west of New Britain Island. Rear Admiral Masatomi Kimura was sure his armada would be covered by fighter aircraft from Rabaul, but his maneuver was detected early on March 1st, and General MacArthur ordered air raids on all Japanese airfields to neutralize Kimura's expected coverage. The Allies waited two days building supplies and practicing for a major attack. On the morning of March 3rd, B-17 and B-24s escorted by American and Australian fighters attacked the Japanese convoy caught in the middle of the Bismarck Sea. The Japanese transports and destroyers scattered in all directions. All of the Japanese transports were destroyed, with at least 3,500 troops either killed or drowned, as well as the cargo meant for Salamaua and other Japanese bases in New Guinea. The Japanese lost ten fighter planes. More Allied attacks were made the next day, while during the night five U.S. patrol-torpedo (PT) boats pursued the stragglers. Out of some 300 aircraft involved, the Allies lost three fighter planes and two bombers and an estimated 20 personnel.

Japan did not attempt another campaign against the Allied troops in New Guinea, and abandoned its troops entrenched along the New Guinea coast. Suffering from hunger, disease, and high casualties, the remaining Japanese became an ineffective force and began retreating toward Finschhafen, Madang, and Hollandia in Dutch New Guinea, to the west.

On September 21, 1943, the Japanese began to flee Lae up the Markham Valley toward Madang on the north coast and up the east coast toward Finschhafen. The Australian 7th Division and U.S. aircraft and ground troops pursued the fleeing enemy up the Markham Valley while the Australian 9th Division pushed the invaders through Finschhafen, but not without a month of fierce fighting, which ended October 20th with the enemy stragglers making it to Madang. Allied personnel took over Finschhafen and immediately began putting the harbor into operation again and building landing fields with grids of pierced steel planking metal sheets placed on the jungle floor. Finschhafen became one of the staging areas for the build-up for General MacArthur's invasion of Leyte in October 1944.

One of the amazing feats of the war in the South Pacific was the display of guts and ingenuity of American servicemen. I was never in the cockpit of a fighter or a loaded C-47 looking down that runway in "Finch," but I would think it would give you pause for reflection and maybe wet drawers to think you had no choice but to try to hit that runway surface so as not to do a flip or sidetrack the plane into the bush. The Army engineers and personnel who scraped dirt and rock and palm trees off soupy surfaces to build landing bases for our airmen deserved a medal of some kind. Coming from a horse economy back in the States, I could not believe the size of the equipment and the unknown possibilities that American boys and men faced in order to get the job done. It was incredible, and most of it had been developed on the spur of the moment back in America and in on-the-job circumstances. It made me proud to be a part of the world's greatest nation whose productive might was unmatched anywhere, thanks to millions of loyal Americans back home.

When I had arrived in Finschhafen in late December 1943, the monsoon season was on and the road through the palm-covered village was nearly impassable. An Army 6x6 truck picked us up at the airstrip and managed to get to our tent area about three miles up the coast. Only high-centered trucks and command cars could negotiate the deep water-filled ruts.

It rained every day for nearly four months. The only road up and down the coast was under water and traffic was near impossible, though ingenious Yankee drivers still managed to figure a way up and down the beaches. Soldiers sloshed back and forth on foot to get to their posts of duty. Less than 10 degrees below the equator, all of coastal New Guinea was a hot, humid, and uncooperative place to live, much less fight an enemy well accustomed to a lesser style of life.

I was assigned tent D-4 where I met my tent mates, Fred, Warren, Jim, and Lou — all Signal Corps men. After getting my bed and gear dried out and my mosquito netting properly hung over my cot, I reported to the 997th Signal Service Center for duty. Every morning and evening I crossed a bank-full stream to get to the Signal Service Center, which was in a huge building with open sides and a thatched roof. It would hold a lot of hay. In the open main part of the building were rows of teletype machines, busy operators, and a message area. After showing me the operations of the Center, the chief operator told me to report back in a couple days.

Back at the campsite, all of the tents were built about two feet off the ground with solid wooden planks for flooring. Tent D-4 was under big, tall, coconut palm trees, supposedly owned by Palmolive-Peat, where the jungle had been pushed aside or felled by shellfire. We were about 100 yards from a white coral beach of the Bismarck Sea. The tent had a skirt of burlap sacking around its base, and even with the heat and high humidity we could survive. There were lots of mosquitoes, but no flies. And it rained . . . and it rained.

One thing bigger than war is the weather. Man cannot change the wet season or the dry. Rain will fall day and night no matter. Average annual rainfall in parts of New Guinea was between 200 and 300 inches. Where did it go? It all looked the same day after day as it ran across the road in front of our tent and into the creek by our Signal Center.

God continued His downpourings as well as His outpourings

accordingly. When the rains come, warlords are forced to put the war on hold. In New Guinea, weeds and flowers continued to cover the ugly ground and the man-made scars of war, and the grass and trees remained bright green and vibrant. The birds and reptiles had fled the beaches. They were smarter than man and survived the downpours. Only man continued his inhumanity to man.

Despite the rain, Papuan natives thrived. They roamed through our campsite almost daily looking for Yankee cigarettes and collectibles. One afternoon while I was in a deep, sweaty sleep on my sagging dilapidated cot along the inside border of our tent, I suddenly awakened with a feeling of someone watching me. Within two feet of my face a pair of squinting, bloodshot eyes peered down at me. A deep guttural sound burst forth from a bushy-haired native leaning against the tent, "Yu got peroxide? Yu got peroxide?" I yanked the mosquito netting back and grabbed my rifle. Then I saw four natives leaning against the tent and grinning at each other. Their teeth and gums were black and red from chewing betel nuts, a hallucinogen. One had his teeth filed to points, giving him the appearance of a man-eating shark.

Awakened from a deep sleep and seeing natives so close to my face, I was unnerved. But their friendly smiles soon convinced me they intended no harm. They wanted the peroxide to streak their big fuzzy hair-dos. The yellow streaks made them socially acceptable and drew the attention of their peers. We gave them some American cigarettes, and they took off for the next tent area.

On one of our trips through the jungle, we were halted by a parade of natives carrying an albino, a native with white-pigmented skin and white hair and eyebrows. He was like a deity to them, and he was protected wherever he went. Even though a war was going on, we had to stop our "Duck" — an amphibious truck codenamed DUKW — to let them cross a jungle trail. Another time, I looked out at the road past the front of our tent and saw four Papuan natives riding in a U.S. military jeep with its shiny black top up. They were dressed in black uniforms and sat stiffly erect, holding Australian rifles and looking straight ahead as they drove past our tent toward the beach. None of us could figure it out. Were they the native police? Who was running the show here?

Every camp had a malaria control specialist. Following headquarters policy, our company had a full-time malaria control soldier who spent each day spraying the surface of puddled water in the tent area. He was a

Two Melanesian wahines relax in their village west of Port Moresby, Papua New Guinea. *Ray Wyatt photo*

The native Papuan police force in Hanuabada village near Port Moresby, Papua New Guinea. These men exhibited unbelievable precision and evidence of training during the South Pacific War.
Ray Wyatt photo

The final resting place for Allied soldiers who had died in New Guinea.
Commonwealth of Australia, Department of Information

The thatched-roof chapel in Finschhafen, New Guinea, along the main road.
Ray Wyatt photo

The author, on the left, with his Army buddies Fred Wade, Max Zanders, and Jim Peterson. *Ray Wyatt photo*

stockily built little guy from New York and a real New Guinea entrepreneur. He subcontracted his job out to a native — pretty good thinking, except that the native brought along his wife and baby. Our man kept them under his bed in the tent area when the other GIs were on duty or elsewhere.

The Signal Corps message center was the large building in the rear. Finschhafen, New Guinea, May 1944. *Ray Wyatt photo*

The author (r) with Max Zanders (l) and Fred Wade (center), outside their tent, D-4, in Finschhafen, New Guinea, August 1944.
Ray Wyatt photo

Australian soldiers in a bomb crater watching for Japanese planes along the coast of Papua New Guinea.
Commonwealth of Australia, Department of Information

American troops had come ashore along the northern coast of New Guinea in April 1944.
Commonwealth of Australia, Department of Information

Each day the traffic in the Signal Center's message center increased as the time for the Leyte invasion neared. The build-up for General MacArthur's return to the Philippines had begun. We kept 20 teletypes busy during the daytime and most of the night.

One difference from my duty in the defense of Darwin campaign was that there were no more Japanese air raids. Because of the capabilities of our American-made aircraft, and the skill and ingenuity of our pilots and the manufacturers back home, the Japanese did not risk anymore air raids over New Guinea. I was told I was "bomb-happy," as I was often seen looking up into the sky for planes. I was always tense and heard noises no one else heard — just plain battle fatigue. The threat to our lives there in New Guinea was from snipers and downed Japanese airmen who had survived crashes, and from enemy stragglers along the coast.

One day, in a reflective mood, I thought of the amazing advancements made in communication technology during the short time I had been in the Signal Corps. Back at Fort Monmouth in January 1942, I had trained with a hand-cranked generator wired to a handkey . . . very primitive communications. Three years later, on transmitter circuits at Finschhafen, I was sending four messages at once with a four-position keying head to our rhomboid antennas. Of course we could receive only one message at a time on our 20 radio/teletypes receivers, but we could send many messages at once through the keying heads on the teletypes.

Our cryptographers, knowing that the Japanese were able to break our code, developed a "garbled" message that seemingly was impossible to decypher. It consisted of our regular 26-letter alphabet plus the period, comma, colon, semicolon, carriage return, question mark, bell, etc., in random order and never in the same sequence.

Sending "garbled" messages by radio/teletype was no problem. Receiving them caused machines to go bonkers. The bell rang, the return reamed out paper, and exclamation marks danced on the sheets. The machines had to be bolted to the floor. The Japanese must have wondered what the American dogfaces were up to. It was hard to believe that I was a part of such a tremendous development and application of signal technology.

While based at Finschhafen, with time to reflect, on April 17, 1944, six weeks before D-Day in Europe, I wrote home to my Father. It was one of those special letters a son sends to his Dad.

> Look Dad. I have written lots of letters home, but none directly to you. You have no doubt read all of my letters. . . . They contained only routine matter. I guess you have wondered what a son thinks of his dad. I have thought of you quite often while doing my work and while on leave. Little incidents which occur strike a parallel to things you and I have done at home.
>
> Many sons never know their fathers. Many never miss them 'till they're gone. Some, unfortunately, have never seen their fathers. So before another world claims you, I want to tell you what I think of you while you are still with us.
>
> First, the way I know you as a man. When I was a little boy, I was with you constantly whether it be under the hot sun at work, or in the evenings by the fire. I was your constant shadow. You were just a "Dad" then and I accepted your guidance and protection as mere formality. Today I know just what it means and the value of a father's guidance. Today I realize how much of a man you were, how well you watched my inquisitive steps, how never once you gave me a bad example, how hard you worked to keep me in clothes and my body healthy, how you never asked for quarter once you set your intentions on a job to be done, how you believed in promptness and initiative, strict and intent, when a job was needed to be done. These are the qualities that made you a man in the eyes of your son. You have strength of character and will-power to do right and keep you word. These are the qualities of a man and not a weakling.
>
> Secondly, the way I know you as a father. You corrected my habits. You were rather severe in your corrections. You were gentle when the job was well done, or new to me. But most of all, you let me find things out for myself. You gave constructive criticism instead of scoldings. You were broadminded for you understood my nature and character and didn't restrict me, but let my qualities develop freely, correcting me only when the bad qualities showed stronger. You watched my language and habits and corrected them, never setting a bad example.
>
> And lastly, though you probably didn't understand all the

intricacies (or idiosyncrasies) of religion, you had a fundamental belief in God and [were] appreciative of His blessings. You didn't understand the divine mysteries of the Holy Trinity, but you had faith in their power to help mankind. You knew that God sent the good days and the bad days accordingly. And now that I am a man, I can appreciate just how much a man you were. How much will power and righteousness you possessed, for I remember you never failed to go down on your knees to say your evening prayers. Something you weren't ashamed of, something that makes you more a man than you are really aware of.

If when I take my place in this world, I am half the man you are, then I need not worry of failure. You've left me a good example. You've gave me a good solid start. I'm a lucky son to have you for a father. You've been all a father could be. For that I will always be indebted to you. May I never bring disgrace on your head. You've given me the right start in life. I want you to feel that you can depend on your son and to feel assured he will be the man you taught him to be. And if his life is claimed by the enemy's bullet and you never see him again, I want you to know he died a man.

Your Son

The regular routine at Finschhafen continued, and chow time was very much a part of that regular life of a soldier. In New Guinea it was also a time for GIs to take atabrine tablets to suppress malaria. At first, we simply followed orders published on the company bulletin board explaining the necessity of keeping less people off of sick call and out of the medical tents. However, some new Signal Corps replacements fresh from the States to our unit believed that taking four or five atabrine tablets each day was a way to get a quick trip back to the States. Too much atabrine brings on yellow jaundice — the medical authorities would want nothing of that! The new recruits rumored that the solution then would be that they would be put on a plane for hospitals in the USA. However, the military quickly figured out the scam, and their solution was to limit the number of pills being taken each meal. So Military Police were stationed at every mess hall to enforce these new regulations. I saw guys so loaded with atabrine that the whites of their eyes and skin turned dark yellow. Naturally, they were convinced they were the smart ones — they would be going right back to the States. They didn't realize the price they were paying.

Despite the sticky heat and mosquitoes, after the monsoon rains let up I managed to explore the beaches and jungle vastness in Finschhafen on Sundays and days off. I wrote in my journal about one of those escapades the same day it happened.

NATIVE DANCE

Finschhafen, New Guinea

October 15, 1944

Along the northern coast of New Guinea on a Sunday afternoon Papuan natives began a ceremonial "sing-sing" in their village halfway up the side of a mountain near our encampment. Knowing that we would likely not have such an opportunity again Corpsmen Fred, Jim, Warren, and I climbed up a nearby mountain through jungle vines and palm trees to watch this unusual fete. As we climbed, we passed a camouflaged spot where the Japanese had built bunkers and gun emplacements to repel Australian troops a few months before. At the base of a tall coconut palm tree I found a Japanese sniper's shoe used to climb trees. The toes on the shoe were separated in the middle like a cow's or goat's foot for easy climbing. It was a prized possession, so much so it suddenly disappeared from my bag.

After climbing the side of the mountain some distance we turned and looked back down at our tent area along the beach. The view was breathtaking. Like a picture post card enlarged 1000 times, a beautiful blue sea framed by white cumulus clouds stretched out toward the New Britain Islands on the horizon. It was hard to believe men were intent on killing each other in this tropical wonderland.

As we cleared the top of a small mesa we saw a village in a clearing of what had been trees and jungle. Our attention was drawn to a group of native men dancing in perfect rhythm. They looked like a drum and bugle corps back in the States. They were lined up four across and six rows deep. From the rear of the columns two drummers beat a fast staccato. I stared in amazement at the perfection and intensity of their dance. The unison of their motions and guttural utterances were unbelievable. After all they were not supposed to be so civilized. I thought, "How did they do that? Who taught them their choreography? Who scheduled their practice for what they did took practice. How did they qualify to be in the group?" What organization and unison a group of onetime savages exhibited there on the side of a jungle fastness! I couldn't believe that a group of so-called primitive men with no schooling, no money, no contests, and no audiences could be so precise and so unconscious of the greatness of their performance. When they finished dancing some Yanks gave them cigarettes for their command performance. We moved on toward the center of the village.

All of the huts had thatched roofs and open sides. As we approached we saw women with babies seated in the doorways. Several native men were wearing triangular shaped headdresses for the "sing-sing." They paid little attention to us or the small number of U.S. soldiers milling around the huts. In fact the setting took on the aura of the warm-ups for football games back home. Several GIs were taking pictures. One old chief with a stick through his nostrils didn't like it. He wanted 10 bob (10 shillings in Australian money) for his photo. Our fellows kept taking pictures anyway. He complained that the natives needed rest . . . would dance later. A big native policeman dressed in a blackskirt and carrying an Australian rifle gently moved us back. On a corner near the end of the compound an American nurse stood with three native men having her picture taken. The chief acted like he was going to kill them, saying no white woman should stand near a native. We decided to leave the area and go deeper into the village.

Moving closer to some of the huts I saw Australian rifles at an entrance. A woman was smoking a pipe and a grave was just outside her hut. In the next hut an old man sat alone smoking an odd shaped pipe. I noticed his hair was bushy and black. All the time I was in the South Pacific I didn't see one native with gray hair. Three women, two babies, and several old men occupied the next tent. The bare-breasted women had spindly legs but all appeared to be well nourished.

As we moved along the row of huts of this Papuan village we saw natives cooking something in a big pot. I felt we were imposing on their privacy and wanted to leave. There was very little activity in the village at that time so we decided to return to our tent area. A native policeman told us we were too early for the big sing-sing.

As we started back down the mountain to our camp we had our picture taken with a couple of the natives. We stopped to talk to the native policeman. He said, "You come alonga 'sing-sing' Lou-night. Good." — meaning for us to come back at night time.

We asked him, "You see Japanese planes?"

He grinned, "See too much Japanese planes. American shoot down. Too much."

With that we started down the mountain to our mess hall.

After chow we again climbed up to the native village. When we got there, the natives were already into their dancing. Costumes on some of the dancers were amazing. In the clearing we could see several groups with immense big headdresses that looked like they were made of cardboard and strips of tin onto which they had daubed paint and colorful bird feathers. Around the outer perimeter of the dancers were several Marys with babies in their arms.

In the center of the main dance arena I estimated there to be 50 to 60 natives. One dancer had an American cigarette stuck in a hole in his ear like a pencil. Others had holes in their noses; some were in costumes made of grass; nearly all had paint on their bodies. One amazing outfit of Japanese paper was worn by a male. Other costumes were highlighted with long bird feathers and strips of gauze painted red; some were of ochre colored bamboo. I saw a lot of Wrigley gum wrappers, and Camel and Lucky Strike cigarette labels imbedded in massive headdresses. An Australian soldier told us that it was a puberty dance for both boys and girls.

During the dance the boys formed an aisle down which the Marys walked in single-file. After completing a walk-through they circled and repeated the ritual while beating on mess kits and gallon cans. This continued with girls going around the ring together, but not touching one another. It was a well-planned but sweaty event. The dance continued for several hours and eventually the sun began to set behind the tree-lined jungle. I never knew when it ended; it had been so repetitive. When the crowd began to disperse we decided to go back to our camp.

As we turned to leave we saw our native police friend standing straight and tall in front of a big stockade, a native calaboose. We asked him about some of the inmates milling around inside the stockade. He said, "Natives in calaboose for stealing and fighting, and pom-pom Mary."

Pointing at one I asked, "What him do? Wha time belonga in the calaboose?"

He replied, "Him fight. Bad. Hurt native. Him do one Christmas." (one year)

Then I pointed to another and asked the same question. He said, "That one steal from native in same village. Him maybe 10 moons."

"What about Mary?" We pointed to a woman walking among the men.

"Mary like native man. Too much. Man pom-pom Mary too much."

"How much time Mary get?"

"Maybe 3 moons." I realized this was the natives' justice system.

Severe punishment for stealing and fighting and lesser for societal actives.

Since it was beginning to get dark and no way to see the trail we began our way down the mountain. We waved to our big friend and moved out. He ran after us and said, "Amee-reeca . . . Good."

We yelled back at him, "You come alonga camp belonga other side road . . . tomorrow noon. We give you American cigarettes. Good."

He said, "Amee-reeca. Good!"

With that we made our way down the mountain to our camp.

Some months later, after returning to the States, I was asked to talk before a college anthropology class. It wasn't until then that I felt the impact of what I had seen in that native village, and the meaning of the sentences given the inmates of that native calaboose. I explained to the class that the surest way to break up a society is to fight with one's fellow man and to steal his property. In the native civilization these crimes would destroy the society. The sins of Mary in that jungle village did not threaten the existence or continuance of her people, but promiscuity was a personal form of destruction.

One night a live USO show was performing on a platform built on a rise along the beach. The audience of American servicemen faced toward the New Britain Islands in the background, and the performers faced in toward the dark jungle and mountains. About 30 minutes into the act, the performance was interrupted by gunfire from U.S. naval ships bombarding a target near Rabaul, Japan's main naval base. It was a beautiful sight. Tracers — every fifth shell — arced through the darkness as the naval guns lobbed big shells from miles off shore. Because of the noise on stage, we couldn't hear the ship's guns or the explosions on the island. It was hard to concentrate on the show. What a mixture of war and entertainment that was!

After nearly 30 months overseas, I began to have attacks of anxiety and found it difficult to relax. Sick call was out of the question. What would I tell a freshly arrived Corporal at the entrance to the medic's reception tent?

I was having terrible nightmares and sleepless nights. I was ashamed of being scared and jumpy all the time, and too proud to admit I was losing control. The sound of propeller-driven bombers made me want to seek cover. And the danger of Japanese snipers was always present. Enemy troops left in the jungles after General MacArthur's bypassing tactics were a constant threat. Careless American soldiers were often ambushed and their clothing and weapons taken by hungry, desperate Japanese. Dressed as American soldiers, they were a constant menace throughout the camp.

In Darwin, air raids had been a different kind of war. The threat to my life there was from bombs falling out of the sky. The threat in New Guinea was different, and from dangers on the ground. In Finschhafen we did not carry weapons to work. We left them stacked against the center pole of our tent for quick retrieval. I developed almost uncontrollable feelings of anxiety and exhaustion from fear of the unknown.

After chow one quiet evening as darkness settled in under the palm trees, a bunch of us sat talking in front of our tent. All of a sudden gunfire interrupted the scene. We knew right away it was coming from the transportation camp 100 yards down in the jungle. In the gathering darkness some Japanese wearing U.S. Army fatigue clothes raided a mess hall. After gaining the entrance, they made for the big breadbox about 10 yards from the door. We heard later that the mess Sergeant saw them and threw a meat cleaver at them, sticking it into a center pole. The Japanese were the only ones with guns. They fired into the air as a diversionary action, while their cohorts grabbed the bread. By the time they left with their loot, several GIs had grabbed guns from their tents and were looking for the Japanese in the darkness. More gunfire . . . only this time more dangerous. The GIs shot at anything that moved. Even our tents were unsafe.

A comforting sight over us, however, were the P-38 Lightning pursuit planes going out to provide cover for our bombers, or just to strafe Japanese left in pockets along the coast, as General MacArthur's leapfrog tactics began to pay off. And we watched dark, silent P-61 Black Widow planes, flying low over the tops of the palm trees at dusk, going out to harass Japanese shipping or known airbases in the Bismarck Sea. I thought the enemy had to be completely demoralized by the apparent superiority of the U.S. equipment now operating in the war. The Japanese had not developed new or surprising stuff during the entire time they had occupied the islands. However, I was told that some American A-20 fighter/bombers had 75 millimeter cannons installed in their nose to see if it could be done. It must to have produced a helluva jar in the cockpit of those planes.

The big day came, when the immense force of men, ships, and planes moved out for the invasion of Leyte, led by General MacArthur. He had waited and planned the exact time and location to announce to the people of the Philippines, "I have returned." As the second and third waves of U.S. military raced toward the Leyte beach on October 20, 1944, back in the Signal Center in Finschhafen we communicated with signal operators on board the landing craft. I remember everyone stopped as we heard desperate "Mayday" calls on voice radio, but the teletypes continued to chatter and get out the messages.

The Battle of the Leyte Gulf, which was a surprise in its intensity and magnitude, turned out to be the last big naval battle of World War II in the South Pacific. Both sides lost a lot of men and equipment, but the Allies proved their superiority on land and on the sea.

Around this time, General MacArthur had issued a bulletin saying all

JUNGLE ROT

Advisory Officer
Lt. H. J. Tucker
Detachment "E"
Ed. b. copeland

997 SIG SVC BN
APO 713-

Mimeograph -Silverman
Dist. - Boris Cohen
997th Signal
Service Bn.

VOL. 1 — Thursday, March 22, 1945 — NO. 13

Edited at Lae, N.G.

MY OUTFIT

The *Jungle Rot* newspaper of the 997th Signal unit at Lae, New Guinea.

men with 24 months overseas were eligible for return back to the States. By November 1944, I had had 30 months — more than enough. When I checked at Company Headquarters for confirmation — surprise! The small print said I had to have a trained person to take my place before I could be placed on the list. But all the new Signal Corps replacements sent to New Guinea had been assigned to MacArthur's task force for the Leyte invasion. It looked like I was in for the duration.

Before Christmas 1944, my Mother began writing that Dad was not well. She had called on the American Red Cross to see if either my brother or I could come home to help out. I asked my Company Commander to help me contact a Red Cross representative in New Guinea to present my request to return home. Nothing happened. Then on January 10, 1945, I was suddenly transferred to the U.S. Army Signal Center back in Port Moresby. I had jungle rot on both hands and legs and a funny shiny scale on the shin of my right leg. The CO said I would get better treatment down at Port Moresby. He got rid of his problem, and I had no recourse but to follow orders.

At Port Moresby I was put in charge of a stand-by radio station making infrequent contact with Finschhafen. Our military encampment was four miles west of the city that at the beginning of the New Guinea campaign had been so active and important to both sides. My tent was on top of a knoll where I could see the entire camp and the surrounding landscape. Moresby was now like a retirement community. There was nothing to do. Communications was a one-man operation and just a job. I became more anxious to get home; my work wasn't really essential any longer, and I knew my Mother needed me. I remember some nights standing outside the radio shack looking up at the myriad of stars and the Southern Cross in the skies over Australia thinking it all seemed a hopeless situation.

Then one morning the monotony was broken by an interesting native. A young Papuan boy dressed in just a sarong appeared in the flap of my tent. His name was Joe Fay. This is his story from my journal:

Joe Fay — Papuan native boy

January 17, 1945

The native men of New Guinea are the unsung heroes during the war in the Southwest Pacific. As subjects of the Australian Government they served their country as part of a Native Police force, carry out "work details," and even transported wounded Allied soldiers back to medical stations during the battles for the Kokoda Trail and the Lae and Buna-Gona campaigns. These natives serving as stretcher bearers were called "Fuzzy Wuzzy Angels" by the Australians for their gentleness and dedication under fierce battle conditions. As a staff/sergeant and the only Signal Corpsman in the Port Moresby area, I was granted special treatment in the form of a native valet. That is how I got to know Joe Fay, a Papuan native boy from Yule Island near Kairuku in the Coral Sea.

When Joe parted the flaps of my tent that morning I didn't know who he was or that the CO had authorized him. As all 5 feet 6 inches of him stood there wearing a big smile, I tried not to look surprised and said, "Wha' name belonga you? You come alonga Hanuabada?"

He came back with, "Speak English. I'm savvy." After that he told me he was to be my "Number One boy." He said he would be my helper on certain days and return each evening to Hanuabada, a native village west of Port Moresby set up for native work forces.

Joe Fay was a small fellow and may have been in his early 20s. He was very polite and a very good worker. He helped me wash clothing and clean up around my tent area. Natives had no way of knowing the titles of officers or leaders in the war but they could sense who was the top guy in most cases. Joe referred to the President of the United States as "Your Number One boy." Officers or top sergeants in our outfit were "Number One boys." In fact I was a "Number One boy."

For a pack of cigarettes he kept me supplied with bananas and paw-paws. His father was Chief Wairopi of a small group of natives on Yule Island some 60 miles up the western coast from Port Moresby. Joe was sent to Moresby under a mandate of the Australian government requiring young natives to serve so many Christmases before being issued money. It was like conscription in the United States. He said he had one Christmas to go before he could return to his island. He was paid in special New Guinea coins . . . about the size of a quarter with a hole in the center and worth about one shilling in Australian money.

One morning Joe came running into my tent shouting, "Look! Look!" He pointed down the hill toward our latrine in a small clearing. I ran out to see what he meant. Cutting across a grassy open space between the latrine and the edge of the woods was a beautiful bay horse. Another with a sleek, brown coat was looking at us with ears held erect and nostrils flared. When it gave a soft neigh Joe grabbed my arm. These splendid animals were said to be from an Australia race track according to company officers who also saw them. They had been sent to New Guinea to assist in moving equipment through the jungles where motorized equipment bogged down in mud and jungle brush and where much of the fighting was hand-to-hand. Some officers had the idea that horses could go where vehicles couldn't. The fighting was fierce and the Japanese had to be gouged out of holes and bunkers on a man to man basis under rainy, mud clogging conditions. When it became evident that using horses in the jungle was not a good idea, these beautiful animals were released to roam at will along the southern coast of New Guinea. I found the present sight incredible. But there before our eyes were two beautiful horses.

Joe Fay had never seen a horse, much less an animal bigger than he. One of the horses stood erect with its head up looking right at us. Then it dropped its head and began eating the thick grass. Joe's hand trembled as he slid behind me. This was an ordinary thing for a farm boy, but to him it was a threat to his life. I told him these animals were used to cultivate the land as well as to fight wars in my country. He seemed to understand.

Joe was needed more in other areas so I requested he be returned to Hanuabada near the harbor of Port Moresby.

At Port Moresby I kept a 16-hour watch on the standby CW circuit handling a few routine messages. The war was moving on. There was no need for urgent communications anymore. When I realized what was happening, I developed an intense dislike for Army life, and officers in general. I felt unnecessary there, and I was desperately needed at home. I was in a terrible, feel-sorry mental state. I was eligible for discharge back in the States, but I couldn't get through to anyone. Letters from home didn't help.

One Sunday morning I went to Mass in a tiny thatch-roofed church situated on a hill overlooking Port Moresby's big harbor. The simple statues and altar decorations inside were beautiful and showed personal caring by someone. The soil was packed hard from many bare feet. There were no kneeling benches or seats. Instead, horizontal poles were placed for leaning one's elbows while standing or kneeling on the dirt floor. In the congregation were a few American and Australian servicemen, plus the local natives and civilians. What set the small gathering apart from the ordinary were a dozen or so Papuan natives wearing simple skirts and red hibiscus blossoms in their beautiful fuzzy hair. It was such a friendly, comforting place that I lingered after the service to visit everyone. As I left, I looked for a souvenir pamphlet or paper that would have the words Port Moresby or New Guinea on it. There on a log near a holy-water dish were carved the words, "Kilroy was here." I was amazed. Kilroy went to church too?

The view that morning of the calm waters of Port Moresby's harbor and the Coral Sea was one I'll never forget. Meanwhile, back at the Army camp, my fourth monsoon season was about to end and the "dry" begin. My hands were sweaty and my anxiety level kept me from resting, even though my job was not a high priority anymore. I awoke exhausted, feeling that my life was out of control most of the time.

On April 14, 1945, President Roosevelt died. The Marines had taken Iwo Jima and they were battling for Okinawa. Men were killing each other in bigger numbers. There was a mix-up in my mail at Finschhafen, and I didn't hear from my Mother or my sisters for two weeks.

Germany surrendered on May 8, 1945. I thought that maybe now my brother would be sent home from Europe. He was married and had a baby girl he had never seen. And Mom needed one of us. Everyone felt that the Japanese couldn't hold off the Allied forces much longer. Maybe I could go home soon.

Then one morning two of my tent mates from D-4 in "Finch" called on a weak radio-telephone hookup and offered condolences. Not fully alert, I asked what for. They seemed surprised and said, "Don't you know your dad died?"

They felt badly, and I was in shock. I went back to my tent and sat on my cot. I thought of Mom alone on the farm with no help. My sisters didn't know how to even hitch up the equipment. My emotions gave way. I walked into the CO's tent and blew my top. I accused the officers — no one in particular — of killing my dad.

I had never lost control of myself before. Ashamed, I left his tent. I had made my point, but I had lost self-control. It was a terrible feeling.

At mail call I received a kind and comforting letter from my D-4 tent-mates in Finschhafen:

May 23, 1945.

Dear Ray:

I hardly know how to start this letter to you. I heard today about your loss of your father. I was hoping you could get home before that happened. We fellows here feel your grief with you for you are one of us. We know your situation.

You have told me your intimate thoughts as a brother. I know your thoughts and feelings. There is one thing though. I know you have learned to take the hardships of life and not let them get the best of you. Just hang on to that ability no matter how hard its seems. Soon you will be going home.

You are now the head man of your family. Your mother will learn to depend on you and that way will help fill the emptiness in her heart for her great loss.

My prayer is that soon the whole world will see the folly of this bloody conflict and will turn back to a decent human way of living. We have all suffered grievous wounds that only time can heal.

Ray, I know you will stick it out and there will be brighter days for you very soon now. As soon as possible you start a family of your own. They are a great comfort in times of trials.

So long for now. Your buddies.

Fred
Warren
Lou
Jim

Back in Kansas, the Red Cross had sent both telegrams of Dad's death to my brother in Europe, adding to my stress. Usually fathers lost their sons to a war. I felt I had lost my father to the war. Pressures were building in me, and I knew I had to get home while I still had control of mind, body, and spirit.

Seeing that I had 35 months overseas, the Captain took action. On May 25, 1945, orders were issued at Port Moresby, returning me back to the United States. I was sent back to Finschhafen, a port of embarkation, and readied for shipment back home. The struggle to get home had been exhausting. I weighed only 137 pounds and couldn't think rationally.

Surely now I could change course and get the energy to live a productive life back in the States where I left off. I remembered the special letter I had written to my father the year before, grateful I had done so.

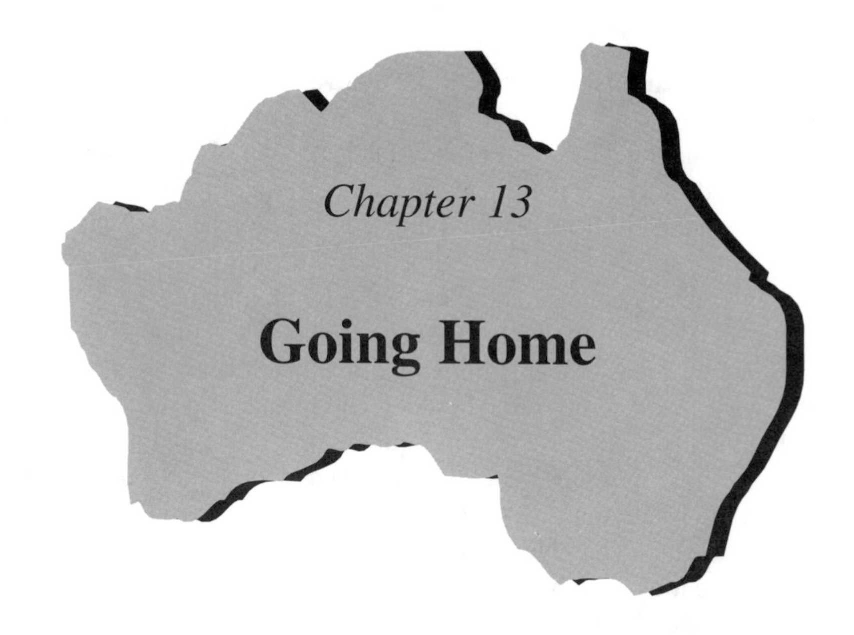

Chapter 13

Going Home

BY MID-MAY 1945 the war was over in Europe. All of the U.S. military power was focused on the Japanese on Iwo Jima and Okinawa, and Japan's mainland. The logistics of supplying millions of men and moving tons of equipment and ammunition into that one focal point is beyond comprehension. Over 1,000 naval vessels were involved. It is impossible to calculate the number of servicemen from all of the Allied forces that converged into that one part of the world. The war couldn't go on much longer. Surely Japan would surrender soon.

One of my last missions of the war had involved a trip to a little island in the Coral Sea called Yule near Kairuku, along the southern coast of New Guinea. The CO at Port Moresby wanted me to check out the possibilities of installing an antenna and radio station on the island.

Before dawn one morning another GI and I were on a small barge with some Australian civilians headed west along the coast in relatively calm water. We had no shade and only our canteens of water and some K-rations. Around mid-afternoon we went ashore on a small dock on Yule Island. Only a few natives greeted us, and we soon made our way up a hill to a small group of huts about a quarter mile from the dock. At sundown the chief of the island and four of his natives visited us and invited us to tour the island the next morning.

Back down the hill from our hut I noticed a mission building and a high wall; evidently missionaries were already established there. A few native women brought us melons, and along with our K-rations, we had some nourishment. We soon found that sleep or even rest was impossible due to the mosquitoes. I was probably bit more often there than at any time in the South Pacific. We had not brought along any means of protection. It was the only time my defense against mosquitoes was down and inadequate.

Early the next morning we joined the chief with about a dozen other natives on the island tour, making notes as to areas that would accommodate a radio setup. The chief understood our assignment and was a gracious host. He took us to his own hut built on stilts in a clearing. He let me climb the steps to his room, which was lined with bamboo. He slept on a mat of kunai grass. It was simple; and it was inspiring. You never see furniture or stoves or white man's tools in a native hut. We thanked the chief for the tour.

On the way back to the docks, we passed a makeshift pen holding several mother pigs and their litters. The chief explained they were highly prized and protected for their meat. Later, I bought a genuine grass skirt with colored braids from a native in exchange for a package of cigarettes. When we finally left the docks that afternoon, natives had brought melons and other vegetables, thinking we would buy them.

The best memory I have of that trip was the beautiful sunset and the singing of those natives as we moved out across the calm water back toward Port Moresby. When I got back to my tent I noticed that the orders the Captain had given me did not set a date for our return — just return on completion of the mission. I could still be there on Yule Island in the Coral Sea. But not likely.

This was at a time before I had received the official orders to return home, and I was anxious to get to my tent because I thought I might have a letter from Mom or the Red Cross, indicating I would be reclassified and sent stateside. No such luck.

All the time I was overseas, letters from home were very infrequent. Most of my mail was from my mother and older married sisters. Mom was kept busy writing because there were four of us kids in the service: my older brother, Joe, was in Europe with the 163rd Combat Engineers with the 7th Army (his outfit built the first pontoon bridges across the Rhine at Remagen); an older sister, Dorothy, was a Major in the Army Nurse Corps; and my youngest sister, Jeanette, was in the Navy WAVES (Women Accepted for Volunteer Emergency Service) stationed on Bremerton Island near Seattle. Besides writing to all of us, Mom was extremely busy keeping the farm running, despite the shortages of gas, tires, sugar, etc., during the rationing days. Toward the end of the war, I received a few V-Mail letters. The lightweight V-Mails could take the place of tons of regular mail and be easily flown to overseas destinations.

Joe wrote to me only once, but after we got together at home, I understood. He had entered France at Cherbourg on D-Day plus 10, and his outfit was at the front all the way to Bavaria and through to the end of the war in Europe May 8, 1945.

With my long-awaited orders in hand, that 25th of May, I stuffed everything I owned into my A-bag: sea shells, some brass casings of spent shells, a miniature lakatoi (canoe), and native combs. Once again I climbed aboard a C-47 for Finschhafen. At a staging area for returnees, 20 other soldiers and I were loaded onto a small boat and ferried out to the *Hughie L. Scott*, a sleek-looking Coast Guard cutter waiting in the quiet waters of the harbor. I was finally leaving New Guinea.

After the ship pulled out into the ocean, I looked back at the New Guinea coast where I had spent nearly 18 months. I was amazed how beautiful the tree-lined shores looked there in the harbor. But I didn't want to go back.

The *Hughie L. Scott* was a modern ship with an upbeat crew. And why not? They were running an escort service in safe waters. The ship was loaded with some 1,000 weary, battle-fatigued, but happy troops. Life aboard ship was wonderful, and the chow was good. There was no pressure to do anything except sleep and eat and listen to the crew's stories of life in the United States. The ship kept an open microphone for anyone who wanted to talk about their experiences, either humorous or serious. I took a turn singing some of the favorites old songs I remembered before the war.

We crossed the International Date Line on May 27, 1945, and headed for Pearl Harbor, where we docked on a cloudy afternoon. We were not allowed to go ashore, but who cared. After a couple of hours in port, our ship headed again for San Francisco and home.

We left Pearl Harbor before sundown, and a heavy overcast moved in over the Pacific. Big ocean swells made the going rough. At midnight the ocean suddenly became full of ships moving in both directions. Navy signalmen blinked messages that lit up the night, until it seemed like Times Square on New Year's Eve. I tried reading their blinkers, but because of the tossing of our ship I gave up. No one slept much that night, and the next morning we were in calm, clear waters, headed for San Francisco.

We put in at Angel Island in San Francisco Bay, and I don't remember much of my first sighting of the California coastline or of going under the Golden Gate Bridge. Angel Island was a staging area for returning soldiers on their way to discharge bases across the United States. We were given another "short-arm" inspection — reminiscent of the day we were inducted — and time to find our bags. I was worried that I would not pass inspection because I was so thin and haggard looking. I had taken so many atabrine tablets for control of malaria that my toenails had developed a purple tint, and the whites of my eyes were yellow. I had to struggle to carry my A-bag off the ship. I still had the same A- and B-bags that I had been issued back at Fort Monmouth 37 months earlier. All of my letters, writings, diary, and photographs were in those bags and represented a segment of my life that I did not want to forget.

Shortly after docking, some guys immediately called home. Others wrote letters. Most of us didn't know what to do to kill time. We stood around smoking and talking in quiet groups in anticipation of boarding a group of ferry boats to take us across the bay to the mainland and our homes.

Finally in the early afternoon, we left Angel Island and loaded onto three long railway coaches destined for discharge centers in the central U.S. Because of my rank as a Staff Sergeant, I was put in charge of all returnees that were to going to Kansas, Nebraska, and Arkansas — one big coach full of soldiers.

When our troop train passed through stations in California, there were few civilian cheers, but everybody on the train was in good spirits. After 24 hours, however, the scene on the train changed and some soldiers became unruly and loud. At one point, out in the Arizona desert, the train stopped to take on water. Contrary to orders, soldiers piled out of coaches and made a dash for a couple of small stores located on the edge of a little town. The train began to move out before all of them could return to their cars. Naturally, those who couldn't make it back to their home car loaded onto whichever they could. We were one of those "whichever" cars, and the last one. After two or three stops for water, our coach was overloaded. By the time we reached the western border of Kansas, we were one over-crowded, stinking, rowdy mess, and a few fights had broken out during the night.

But just being back in my home state was wonderful, and I felt better already. As the train moved along the tracks, soldiers hung from every window. We yelled and waved as we passed through each town. The train slowed to a snail's pace when we passed through the suburbs of Ottawa, Kansas. One of our passengers was from Ottawa, and we gave him a special window so he could take it all in. His home was by the tracks and he was going to give out a big whoop when he went by his backyard in hopes his wife would be there and see him. Imagine his surprise when he saw her in his backyard, but with a guy he knew. We had to hold onto his legs to keep him from going right out the window. He was fit to be tied for the rest of the trip.

At Kansas City's Union Station, soldiers from our coach found their way back to their former coaches for the remainder of their trip — one going to Camp Chaffee, Arkansas, and another to Fort Leonard Wood, Missouri. From Kansas City, my section of the train went to Fort Leavenworth. It was carrying only 75 percent of our original complement because some enterprising GIs had jumped off the train in Kansas City and took taxicabs clear to Fort Leavenworth just to beat the train!

I was discharged at noon on July 9, 1945, at Fort Leavenworth, two months short of four years after my enlistment. Mustering-out pay was $287. Once again I was a free man.

I bought a ticket to Atchison aboard a Missouri Pacific train and checked both of my Army duffel bags in the baggage car. As that beautiful passenger train moved along the west bank of the Missouri River toward Atchison, I felt some peace returning to my soul. As if it were meant to be, someone's radio was playing "Sentimental Journey." I began to feel I was home . . . at last!

One of my sisters and several nieces were at the Union Station in Atchison to greet me. There was no fanfare. No cheering. No returning hero. No big deal. Mom was waiting for me in the living room of my sister's house in north Atchison. We hugged and hugged for a long time. That afternoon, one of my sisters took Mom and I home to the farm south of Effingham, 17 miles west of Atchison. It was great to be home. The lane looked the same. The yard light was still in place, but the barn needed painting. I sat down to Mom's good cooking, but couldn't eat.

Adjusting to civilian life and pumping up the will power to make a living on my own were my immediate challenges. The world had not waited on the soldier, but had moved on at a bewildering pace. The war against the Japanese was still going on in the Pacific and there was just Mom and me to listen to radio broadcasts of the action.

I had to begin again where I had left off, but without the help and counsel of my dad. But first, I had to get my strength back and reconcile my thoughts about the world I now faced.

Once-familiar sounds on the farm seemed so strange now, after the jungles of New Guinea, and I awoke at night wet in a sweat. The war was still going on in my head.

Chapter 14

America the Beautiful

IN JULY 1945, I walked back up the same country lane I had left nearly four years earlier. But it was a bittersweet experience. I was happy to be alive. I had a place to which I could return. But Dad wasn't there. Home was so empty without him.

My neighbor was cutting a field of alfalfa. I had forgotten the wonderful odor of freshly mowed hay. It was hot and humid, like I had remembered Kansas in July. Big cumulus clouds were beginning to form over the countryside that afternoon. It was great to be back.

At the time of my discharge on July 9th my brother Joe was still in Europe. On May 8th he had been assigned guard duty at Hitler's hideout at Eagle's Nest in Germany. My sister Dorothy, in the Army Nurse Corps, was in Denver, and my youngest sister, Jeanette, was still a WAVE.

Dad had died just two months before I got home. Mom had paid a man in his 70s to do the morning milking, and a high school boy did the chores each evening on his way home from school.

There was a lot of field work to do, but it seemed that all I got done was milk the cows and do the other small chores each day.

Then one afternoon, in mid-August, Mom and I heard the news on our radio that Japan had surrendered. The actual signing of the surrender took place on September 2nd, on board the USS *Missouri*. The war that began with such aggression by the Japanese ended in a defeated and subdued people.

I was relieved that the bloodshed was over, but I was bitter. So many millions of our country's finest young lives had been lost and so much property destroyed because of the greed of a few leaders.

Reality was beginning to set in for me. I had no job, very little money, and no car. I had no skills. The farm wasn't a money-making deal. Dad had all horse-drawn equipment and had been too sick to take care of it. Weeds around the barnyard and chicken house had grown as high as the proverbial elephant's eye. The lane was full of ruts and needed grading. I didn't recognize any of the horses or milk cows, and there were none of my favorite animals around. There was just Mom and me — and memories. I soon realized I was not up to par mentally or physically for the challenging new responsibility that confronted me.

The sunny weather during August 1945 was like the days of old on the farm. Because of war demands, wheat prices were better than when I had left in 1941, and I managed to put together enough chewed-up, old harnesses for three horses to pull an old six-foot-cut McCormick binder, and I harvested most of the 25 acres of wheat that Dad had planted back in October 1944.

On one of my first trips to town, I didn't recognize many of the people. Even the alley dogs looked a little strange. Most of Effingham's businesses were on Main Street, which was only two blocks long. The population was 604 when I left in 1941. With most of the young men gone, it was a lot less now. One old man, a World War I veteran, hugged me with tears in his eyes as we stood in front of Abe's Cafe, the main feed-trough before the war. Mike Meador's Saloon smelled the same, and a game of dominoes was in progress, as if I had never left. The Hegarty brothers still ran the only bank in town, and the barber pole was still turning in front of "Paddy" Stewart's shop, where I got my hair cut long ago. But I didn't have enough hair left to warrant even a modest butch.

During the early fall months of 1945, I became increasingly tense and unstable. I began having nightmares and so-called battle dreams. The farm chores didn't let up, and I milked cows each morning and evening, fed the horses and steers, cleaned the cow barns and chicken house, and cut weeds along the roadside and pastures. Mom gave me the 1937 Ford two-door, after I paid a repair bill at Barnett's garage. But she soon realized that I could not take Dad's place. I was in no condition to make a living on the farm. We had to do something before wheat seeding season would begin.

During October, we put together a farm sale and disposed of all the equipment and household items we owned. The weather was nice the day of the sale and a good crowd came to help Mom and wish her well. Following the sale, we bought a two-bedroom home in Atchison, near my older sister and her family.

But my nightmares began again. I continued to hallucinate and awaken drenched with sweat. One morning, when my mother inadvertently touched my leg to awaken me, I awoke fighting and striking out at her.

I knew I had to do something to get help. Flashbacks of air raids in Darwin and snipers in New Guinea haunted me. The more I tried to dismiss them, the more I found myself thinking of them. I was ashamed of being afraid. During the day I began to flashback to conditions as they were in the war. The effects of too many atabrine tablets made me lethargic, and jungle rot began to inflame my fingers and toes from my sweaty hands.

With an accelerating level of anxiety and nagging memories to deal with, I needed help. Finally, I drove 30 miles to Wadsworth Veterans Administration Hospital in Lansing, Kansas. I was admitted in February 1946 and given a barium test. I was told that my stomach had shrunk to about half its normal size, probably due to the dehydrated food served in the mess hall at Finschhafen. I was also given a procedure called "twilight sleep." I remember very little of this except the darkened room and lying on a simple cot against the wall while the doctor asked questions of my overseas experiences. I answered the questions and relived the air raids on the beach at Darwin. I didn't understand why I was participating in this procedure.

Finding no apparent active illness, the doctors sent me home. Yet I knew that my problem was not physical but mental. I knew I was battle-fatigued, scared, and desperate. Most important, I was ashamed to talk about my condition, for fear of what people would think of me. I didn't know where to turn for support, and I worried about taking care of Mom.

Fear and anxiety consumed most of my waking hours. I needed to get employment to get my mind off myself and to make a living. But I needed help to unlock the deep anxiety feelings and bitterness developing in my life.

I returned to the Wadsworth Hospital a month after being discharged, and this time I was put in a ward used primarily for veterans of World War I — the "death ward." Most of the men in it were suffering advanced stages of syphilis. They were not expected to leave the hospital alive. There were bars on my window and the door opened from the outside. Some of those old timers would beat on my door every day and yell foul language at me. My roommate was a young GI from the China-Burma-India Theater of war. But he was in bad shape and was soon removed from the cell. I was alone . . . again.

During this second trip to Wadsworth, I received an average of five shots a day administered mostly in my buttocks. And each morning I was sent to a physical therapy room where an attendant had me stand naked in a tubular shower cage while he played two streams of water, one cold and the other warm, up and down my body. Sometimes he let the pressure build on those nozzles until I could hardly stand erect. After these sessions I returned to my cell exhausted. I did not need physical therapy. I needed psychiatric treatment for my deep anxiety, but who could I talk to that would understand? The Wadsworth Hospital was not prepared for the problems of the World War II veterans they accepted during that fall of 1945, though they did the best they could.

One afternoon the Leavenworth Sisters of Charity saw my name as they checked admissions to that ward. Shortly thereafter a Catholic priest came into my room to hear my Confessions and give me Holy Communion. As he unfolded his little satchel, I looked up at him and said, "What the hell are you doing here, Father?" It was midday and not his usual contact period on the ward. Was I really that near death? It was surely a mistake.

No member of my family, except my mother, was allowed to visit me, but Mom had no way of getting to the hospital. One evening after Taps I heard a young couple under my window talking and laughing as lovers do, and it kindled a desire in me to get well and be loved by someone. I knew I had normal feelings and responses; but I needed help sorting everything out.

Each evening a bugler blew Taps. That had been the most beautiful sound I had heard during all of my Army career. The bugler at Wadsworth played a clear tone that echoed from a large building near my ward. I waited for it each night and from one of the older veterans learned the words:

> Day is done
> Gone the sun
> From the lake
> From the sky
> All is well
> Safely rest
> God is nigh.

Toward the end of the second week at Wadsworth I asked to be discharged and sent home. I was given a hearing with five people sitting in judgment of my request. What a humiliating experience that was. One doctor asked, "What makes you think you are well?"

It's a challenge for anyone to answer that question to the satisfaction of a psychologist! However, I was dismissed.

In an effort to get on the right track, I made the decision to enroll again in St. Benedict's College, just six blocks from home, and one day Father Gilbert asked me to give the talk to his anthropology class about the natives of New Guinea, their lifestyle and their culture. But once again the haunting memories triggered sweaty, nervous periods. I had to drop my classes.

Finally, during the summer of 1946 I got a job with a construction company, building electrical lines along a highway west of Atchison. When the job ended in late summer, I returned to Wadsworth. This time the hospital sent me to Winter Veterans Hospital in Topeka. My papers said I had pyschotaxis of despair and battle stress. At Topeka I got help at last. Winter Veterans Hospital had been developed to treat the battle-fatigue syndrome and stress of World War II veterans. It seemed no coincidence that it was located in the same city as the well-known Menninger's Mental Health Clinic.

My first weeks at Winter Veterans were tough because of my attitude and refusals to talk or cooperate. Many nights I stood on a wooden walk-

Ray Wyatt's sisters, Major Dorothy Wyatt of Army Nurse Corps (l) and Ethel (center), with the author a few weeks after he returned to the farm. (He weighed only 137 pounds.) It was Ray Wyatt's 25th birthday, August 6, 1945, the day the atomic bomb was dropped on Hiroshima, Japan. *Ray Wyatt photo*

way outside my ward and stared out into the night. I developed an unbelievable animosity for anyone who tried to help me. But a wonderful nurse would quietly talk about pleasant things until I returned to my cot on her ward.

Yet, I continued to be uncooperative or take part in therapy classes. Then one morning, after everyone had left the ward, a nice middle-aged farm boy from Nebraska came to my bed and asked if I would go with him to visit the Gray Ladies, a voluntary group in Topeka who worked with hospital staff. I had no idea who they were, but it sounded interesting and I consented.

In a well-lighted room filled with gadgets and colorful paper, a gray-haired, gentle lady asked me if I would help her. Who could refuse? She said she needed to have the threads of a silk scarf pulled apart. She showed me how to pull them apart one thread at a time. When I had finished, there

The author's brother, PFC Joe C. Wyatt, served with the 163rd Combat Engineers in the European Theater.

were two piles of silk thread on the floor. It worked. I was so pleased working with my hands and so engrossed in my job that I began to relax. Each day she helped me. I stenciled a pretty rose onto a silk scarf to give to my mother. Such a simple act of kindness from someone who genuinely cared started me back on the road to recovery.

My treatment at Winter Veterans progressed from pulling silk thread to separating round blocks from square blocks and red objects from blue objects in a playpen for two- and three-year-old children. I played children's games to test my basic knowledge of childhood events and made progress toward recovery. During the summer months I advanced to playing on a piano keyboard, shooting baskets on outdoor courts, and playing golf.

The family military service tradition went back to Albert Scott, Jr., Ray Wyatt's mother's youngest brother. Scott was killed in the First World War in the Argonne Forest after Germany had surrendered and before the Armistice was signed.

During this time I was under the care of Dr. Eugene Goforth, a wonderful psychiatrist. He patiently led me back to my confidence and individual freedom. He asked about my dog, my girlfriend, my parents, sibling order in the family, my prewar buddies. These were "cords," he told me, tying me back to my past while I was overseas and under trying conditions. In most cases, there had been a complete severance of the prewar cords. My dog, Duke, had died when his hind leg caught in the upper strands of a barbed-wire fence and he hung there until he died. My girlfriend had gotten married. My buddy had not gone overseas as expected. And, as a last major cord, my father had died before I got home. All these events had occurred while I was overseas — these plus the fact that I had lost a lot of my physical stamina and vigor. When these "cords," the basic anchors in my life, were gradually severed, compounded with the high level of fear and anxiety overseas, I had too heavy a mental load to augur all at once. Dr. Goforth helped me analyze each anchor in my life and develop solutions.

From the doctor's therapy I reaffirmed important values. He convinced me that I could be a strong individual again.

In the fall of 1946 I enrolled at Kansas State College of Agriculture in Manhattan (now Kansas State University) under the new GI Bill. I met my future wife there and life took on a new meaning. The GI Bill payed my tuition and a $110 per month subsistence. My 50 percent disability paid an additional $57.50 per month. Once again, my country with its guaranteed freedoms and opportunities had come through for me when I needed help the most.

I was able to complete my education and obtain a Bachelor of Science degree in Agricultural Journalism. The future was no longer in doubt. The day after my graduation in June 1949, I was employed by the Kansas Farm Bureau, a voluntary membership farm organization, whose belief in constitutional government, individual responsibility, and the American way of life matched mine exactly. I asked to be taken off disability status for fear of the stigma of being disabled. And then, in January 1948, I married my college sweetheart.

I was fortunate to have served in Australia. Our roots were from England and we spoke a common language and fought for the same principles. I am also grateful for having been born into a large family where I experienced democracy and freedom first-hand on the farm. I had a wonderful father and mother whose guidelines and discipline were a stabilizing force in my life. I knew from whence I had come and for what I had fought. I understand and appreciate my right to be called an American.

My positive association with the people in the Land Down Under was a key to my return to a productive life again after the war. No matter what the hardship or calamity, the Australians would always say, "She'll be right!"

My response to the Australians is, "Gud on ya', Aussie. She'll be right, Mite!"

Afterword

MANY GOOD MEN ARE DEAD — the guys who had to look down the barrel of a gun, light the fuse of the cannons, or drop the bombs because they were servicemen and their country expected it of them. They had to steel their minds, their will, to accept the fact that they were killing another human being, one of God's creatures. They crossed the barrier in their conscience.

All wars are bad. They destroy lives and property. They mangle the human mind, sometimes forever.

President Abraham Lincoln eloquently stated in his address at Gettysburg on November 19, 1863:

> It is for us the living, rather, to be dedicated to the unfinished work that those who died here have so nobly advanced. . . . that we firmly resolve that they have not died in vain.

Alcorta, Frank. *Australian Frontline, The Northern Territory's War.* North Sydney, New South Wales. Allen & Unwin Pty Ltd. 1991.

Barrett, Charles. *Blackfellows: The Story of Australia's Native Race.* Melbourne, Sydney. Cassell & Co. Ltd. 1942.

Binning, John. *Target Area.* Sydney, New South Wales. Australian Publishing Co. Pty. Ltd. 1943.

Bliven, Bruce, Jr. *From Pearl Harbor to Okinawa.* New York. Random House. 1960.

Burns, Michael. *Spitfire! Spitfire!* New York. Blandford Press. 1986.

Christmas, Linda. *The Ribbon and the Ragged Square, an Australian Journey.* New York. Viking Penguin Inc. 1986.

Coe, Lewis. *The Telegraph: A History of Morse's Invention and Its Predecessors in the United States.* Jefferson, NC. McFarland & Company, Inc. 1993.

Department of Veterans Affairs. *Australia Remembers, 1945-1995.* Canberra. Department of Veterans Affairs. 1994.

Drea, Edward J. *MacArthur's ULTRA (Codebreaking and the War against Japan, 1942-1945).* Lawrence, Kansas. University Press of Kansas. 1992.

Dupuy, R. Ernest. *The National Guard, a Compact History*. New York. Hawthorn Books, Inc. 1941.

Fisher, Allan C., Jr. "Australia's Pacesetter State, Victoria," *National Geographic,* Vol. 139, No. 2 (1970): 218.

Hill, Ernestine. *Australian Frontier*. New York. Doubleday, Doran & Co, Inc. 1942.

Historical Office Staff. *A Concise History of Fort Monmouth, New Jersey*. Fort Monmouth. U.S. Army Communications-Electronics Command. 1985.

Johnston, George H. *New Guinea Diary*. Sydney, London. Angus and Robertson Ltd. 1943.

Judge, Joseph. "The Tragic Journey of Burke and Wills," *National Geographic*, Vol. 155, No. 2 (1979): 152.

Lapica, R. L. *Facts on File Yearbooks*. New York. Person's Index, Facts on File, Inc. 1941-1945.

Miller, John, Jr. *Cartwheel: The Reduction of Rabaul*. Washington, D.C., Center of Military History, United States Army. 1990.

Milner, Samuel. *Victory in Papua: The War in the Pacific*. Washington, D.C., Center of Military History, United States Army. 1955.

Moresby, Isabelle. *New Guinea: The Sentinel*. Melbourne, Sydney. Whitcombe & Tombs Pty. Ltd. 1943.

Morrisey, Muriel Earhart and Osborne, Carol L. *Amelia, My Courageous Sister*. Santa Clara, CA. Osborne Publisher, Inc. 1987.

Perret, Geoffrey. *There's a War to Be Won*. New York. Ballantine Books. 1991.

Salmaggi, Cesare and Pallavisini, Alfredo. *2194 Days of War*. New York. Gallert Books. 1979.

Snyder, Louis L. *Louis L. Snyder's Historical Guide to World War II*. Westport, CT. Greenwood Press. 1979.

Webb, Rev, T. T. *Spears and Spades*. Sydney, New South Wales. Spectator Publishing Co. Pty. Ltd. 1938.

Wrixon, Fred B. *Codes And Ciphers*. New York. Prentice Hall General Reference. 1992.

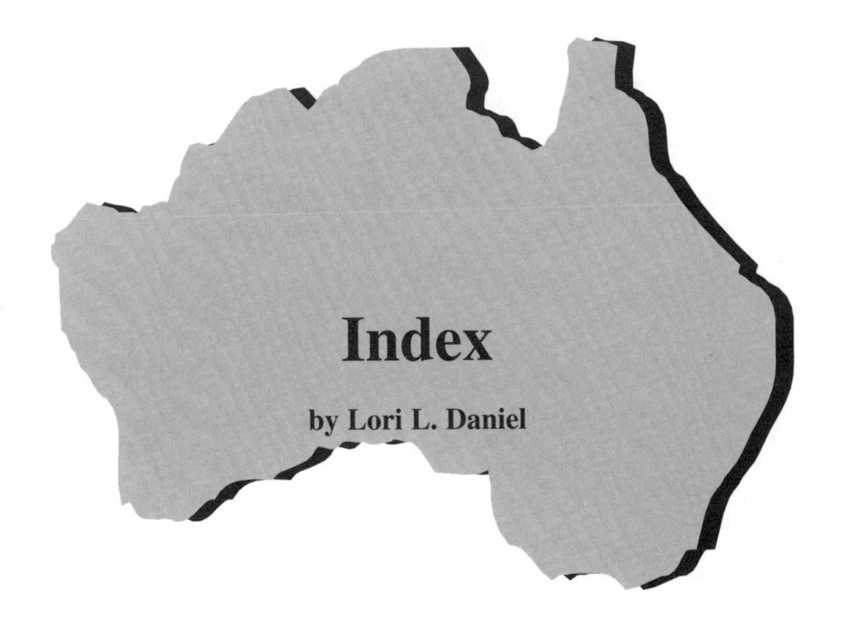
Index
by Lori L. Daniel

— Y —

— Z —